QUICK-QUILTED

Home Decor

WITH

YOUR BERNINA

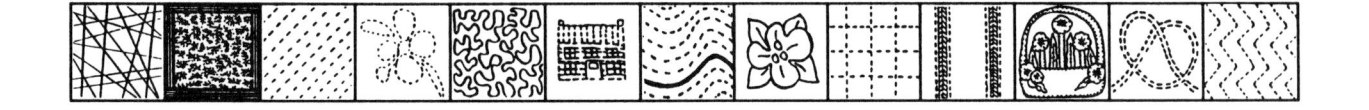

OTHER BOOKS AVAILABLE FROM CHILTON
Robbie Fanning, *Series Editor*

Contemporary Quilting Series

Contemporary Quilting Techniques, by Pat Cairns
Fast Patch, by Anita Hallock
Fourteen Easy Baby Quilts, by Margaret Dittman
Machine-Quilted Jackets, Vests, and Coats, by Nancy
  Moore
Picture Quilts, by Carolyn Vosburg Hall
Precision Pieced Quilts Using the Foundation Method, by
  Jane Hall and Dixie Haywood
Quick-Quilted Home Decor with Your Sewing Machine, by
  Jackie Dodson
The Quilter's Guide to Rotary Cutting, by Donna Poster
Quilts by the Slice, by Beckie Olson
Scrap Quilts Using Fast Patch, by Anita Hallock
Speed-Cut Quilts, by Donna Poster
Super Simple Quilts, by Kathleen Eaton
Teach Yourself Machine Piecing and Quilting, by Debra
  Wagner
Three-Dimensional Appliqué, by Jodie Davis

Creative Machine Arts Series

ABCs of Serging, by Tammy Young and Lori Bottom
The Button Lover's Book, by Marilyn Green
Claire Shaeffer's Fabric Sewing Guide
The Complete Book of Machine Embroidery, by Robbie and
  Tony Fanning
Creative Nurseries Illustrated, by Debra Terry and Juli
  Plooster
Creative Serging Illustrated, by Pati Palmer, Gail Brown,
  and Sue Green
Distinctive Serger Gifts and Crafts, by Naomi Baker and
  Tammy Young
The Fabric Lover's Scrapbook, by Margaret Dittman
Friendship Quilts by Hand and Machine, by Carolyn
  Vosburg Hall
Gifts Galore, by Jane Warnick and Jackie Dodson
How to Make Soft Jewelry, by Jackie Dodson
Innovative Serging, by Gail Brown and Tammy Young
Innovative Sewing, by Gail Brown and Tammy Young
*Owner's Guide to Sewing Machines, Sergers, and Knitting
  Machines,* by Gale Grigg Hazen

Petite Pizzazz, by Barb Griffin
Putting on the Glitz, by Sandra L. Hatch and Ann
  Boyce
Serged Garments in Minutes, by Tammy Young and
  Naomi Baker
Sew, Serge, Press, by Jan Saunders
Sewing and Collecting Vintage Fashions, by Eileen
  MacIntosh
Simply Serge Any Fabric, by Naomi Baker and Tammy
  Young
Soft Gardens: Make Flowers with Your Sewing Machine, by
  Yvonne Perez-Collins
Twenty Easy Machine-Made Rugs, by Jackie Dodson

Know Your Sewing Machine Series, by Jackie Dodson

Know Your Bernina, second edition
Know Your Brother, with Jane Warnick
Know Your Elna, with Carol Ahles
Know Your New Home, with Judi Cull and Vicki Lyn
  Hastings
Know Your Pfaff, with Audrey Griese
Know Your Sewing Machine
Know Your Singer
Know Your Viking, with Jan Saunders
Know Your White, with Jan Saunders

Know Your Serger Series, by Naomi Baker and Tammy Young

Know Your Baby Lock
Know Your Pfaff Hobbylock
Know Your Serger
Know Your White Superlock

Teach Yourself to Sew Better Series, by Jan Saunders

A Step-by-Step Guide to Your Bernina
A Step-by-Step Guide to Your New Home
A Step-by-Step Guide to Your Sewing Machine
A Step-by-Step Guide to Your Viking

QUICK-QUILTED

Home Decor

WITH

YOUR BERNINA

JACKIE DODSON

CONTEMPORARY
QUILTING

CHILTON BOOK COMPANY
Radnor, Pennsylvania

Designed by Stanley S. Drate and Ellen Gleeson / Folio Graphics Co., Inc.

Produced by March Tenth, Inc.

Manufactured in the United States of America

Library of Congress Cataloging-in-Publication Data

Dodson, Jackie.
    Quick-quilted home decor with your Bernina / Jackie Dodson.
        p.   cm. — (Contemporary quilting)
    Includes bibliographical references and index.
    ISBN 0-8019-8369-X
    1. Machine quilting.   2. Machine appliqué.   3. House furnishings.
I. Title.   II. Series.
TT835.D637   1994
746.46—dc20   93-46375
                                                              CIP

1 2 3 4 5 6 7 8 9 0   2 1 0 9 8 7 6 5 4 3

Registered trademarks, and trade names

Aleene's Stop Fraying	Polaroid
Craft Cord	Radio Shack
Fasturn	Sculpey
Fiskars	Styrofoam
Gingher	Sulky
Goop	Tandy
HeatnBond	Teflon
Household Goop	ThreadFuse
Mundial	Ultrasuede
Metrosene	Velcro
Natesh	Wonder-Under
Pellon	

CONTENTS

FOREWORD

Recently my husband bought a vest of many pockets and decided to change it from a button to a zipper front. He's not experienced at sewing, but he's not afraid, either. I explained what to do and pointed him toward my Bernina. Within hours, he had what he wanted—plus a new-found love. "What a machine!" he kept saying.

I do have more sewing experience and I have lots of editing experience, too. Whenever I read one of Jackie Dodson's new books, I keep saying, "What a writer!"

Her books are always jammed with bonus ideas, not just the main project. In *Twenty Easy Machine-Made Rugs* I learned a technique for gathering strips—and now I can use it in smaller scale for texture on a garment. I learned how to use the various presser feet in *Know Your Sewing Machine* and now I have the tools to sew anything. In this book, I stitched her folding book of machine-embroidery stitches and now I have the vocabulary to decorate anything with my beloved Bernina.

Bernina and Jackie Dodson—what a pair!

ROBBIE FANNING
Series Editor

ACKNOWLEDGMENTS

Thank you:

To my mother, Kap Hanson, who showed me what fun it is to make something out of nothing. To my aunt, Helen Ove, whose hands and mind were always creating, and my aunt, Fritz Martin, whose home is an inspiration of hand-made, house beautiful.

To JoAnn Pugh, Sharon Kelly, and Bernina of America, who come to my aid whenever I call them.

To Jan Saunders and Nancy Bednar, for listening, advising, and being on the same wavelength.

To Marilyn Tisol, a special friend, critic, and sounding-board.

And to my editor, Robbie Fanning, for her optimism, encouragement, and endless support.

INTRODUCTION

Why would anyone spend time sewing home decorations when they can buy whatever they need? We all know the answer: Yes, we can buy what we *need*—but we can make what we *want*. There's a difference. For example, I needed curtains for a bedroom window—quick—when friends invited themselves for the weekend, so I decided to buy curtains (a first)—mail-order—to save even more time. Well, they are what I *need*, but certainly not what I *want*. When the curtains arrived, I hated the fabric and their skimpiness. The closest curtain length I could choose was either too long or too short, so these didn't come together in the middle without leaving sides open. I still want to make curtains for that bedroom window.

More and more of us are finding that with new notions, fusibles, drapery tapes, and threads, along with teaching videos, sergers, miracle sewing machines, and gorgeous fabrics, we can custom-make beautiful home decorations quickly. And if we make them ourselves, they'll reflect our tastes, they'll fit, and the price will be right.

Why is there a trend toward home decoration in sewing? A TV reporter had an answer: We are becoming burrowers. One reason for that is we feel safer at home than on the streets. We burrow when we rent videos instead of attending a movie, send out for pizza instead of eating in a restaurant, call a grocery store to deliver our food, order by mail instead of shop at the mall. Even more businesses are in the home. We don't have to go out of the house.

Gerald Calente, a trend researcher for the Socio-Economic Research Institute, claims that the recession is a cause for this stay-at-home attitude. We don't have the money to go out, so we stay at home. It only follows that we want to beautify the surroundings where we spend most of our time.

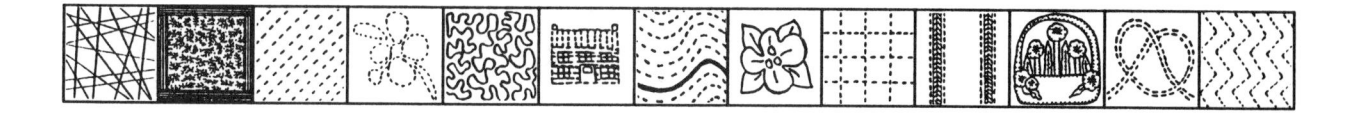

Whatever the reason, the fact remains that we are decorating our homes and doing it ourselves.

Fabric stores are taking the lead with their "home-dec" departments, a term invented in the last couple of years. Today's store devotes more square feet to decorating the home than it did a year ago. Sample curtains, swags, and pillows tempt the do-it-yourselfer, along with new products, books, and pamphlets to help you decorate every inch of space in your home. (Of course sewing and fabric catalogs offer everything needed for decorating [see Sources of Supplies, page 93], and they're delivered to our homes, so all we have to do is fill out an order form, slip it into a mailbox, and go back to our burrows.)

When you read through the projects that follow, you'll discover that this book shows you how to decorate with machine quilting; it's not a book to *teach* you how to machine-quilt. (If you want to learn machine quilting basics, I suggest two Chilton books: *The Complete Book of Machine Quilting*, by Robbie and Tony Fanning, and *Teach Yourself Machine Piecing and Quilting*, by Debra Wagner.)

When I burrow, I love to sew, and quilting by machine is one of my favorite activities. For the little time it takes to decorate with machine quilting, the results are terrific.

The machine-sewn projects in this book are divided into three chapters. Each chapter is a separate decorating style: Victoriana, Cowboys and Indians, and 90s Are Now. The first decorative accessory I show you how to make is a Flower Wallhanging, a sampler of the many ways to machine quilt. Even if you don't make the wallhanging, try all the techniques and place the results in a notebook or on a bulletin board where you can refer to them as you stitch the other projects.

In addition to the sampler there are fourteen other machine-quilted projects: a pastel wallhanging, quilt shred flower garden pillows, sampler book of Bernina stitches, thoughtful pillowcases, leather headboard with pillows to match, decorated and slashed fabric pillows, duvet cover/sum-

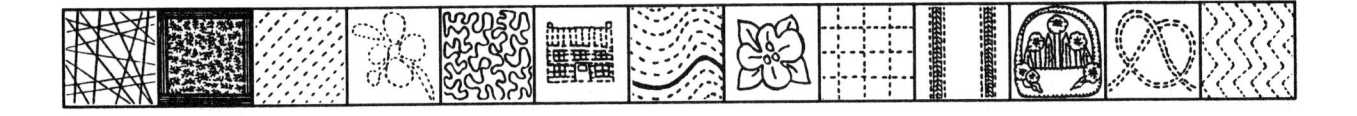

mer quilt with matching pillow sham, and a picnic mat. Along with those projects are others that may or may not be quilted. They are added to coordinate and complement the other accessories in the chapters. There is something for every taste. But if you don't find yourself in one of them, it may take only a fabric change to make it truly you.

More information is included in size charts, sources of supplies, and a bibliography of other home-dec books to keep you busy the rest of your life.

I promised you quick quilting on the sewing machine. Check out Chapter 4, "Quilting/Sewing Shortcuts," page 82, to see how I cut down on construction as well as decorating time, and use these tips and hints whenever applicable in all of your sewing.

This book is a collection of ideas I've played with through the years. Instead of leaving an experiment as only a square of stitching on my sewing table, I've used the ideas for projects, and now you have the benefit of some of those experiments.

Never stop trying new things or you'll miss out on all the fun. Use the ideas in this book as I've shown them, or use them as jumping-off-places for your own experiments. I don't believe in always following directions, and I hope you approach the projects with that in mind. Change them by using your favorite threads and decorative stitches. Choose colors you love, not what someone else tells you is stylish. That's what makes your home look like you. It's also what makes sewing home decor fun.

Pamela Clabburn, of Norwich, England, defines quilting in *The Needleworker's Dictionary*: "The stitching together of two or three thicknesses of fabric to make something which can be warm, protective, or purely decorative." That definition can include appliqué, reverse appliqué, layering sheers and transparencies, and much more. It's fun to stretch the quilting imagination, so let's get to it.

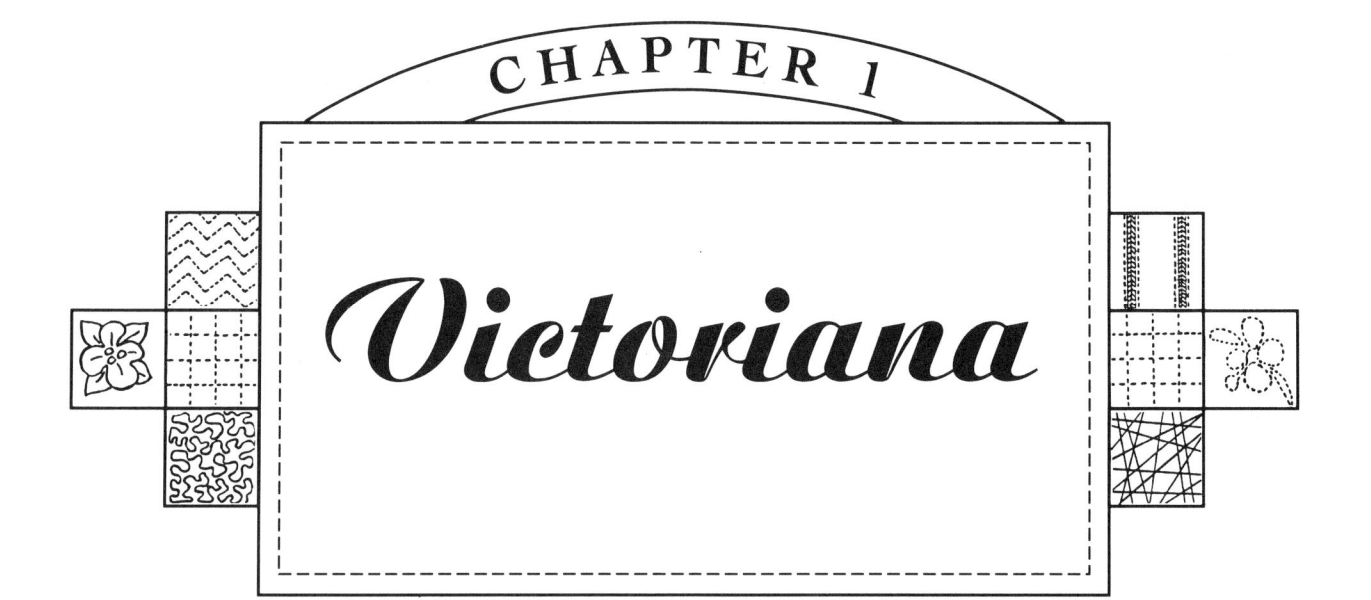

CHAPTER 1

Victoriana

Included in this chapter of Victoriana are lace, pearl buttons, embroidery, and satin ribbons, beginning with a machine-quilted wallhanging, a sampler of machine quilting techniques. It is the one exception to the pastels I chose for the other projects.

The second wallhanging is an easy way to appliqué and quilt at the same time. What I like about each square on this hanging are the two designs I've created: first the collage of colors, then the lines of over-stitching.

You'll also find here a way to resurrect quilt shreds you've relegated to the trash by cutting them into pillow shapes, then covering them with ribbons, cords, lace, buttons, and bridal tulle. Stitched down with decorative machine stitches, the shreds are saved and you've created an heirloom.

I pieced and quilted a book cover for another project. When the cover is opened, a long strip of stitch samples from my Bernina 1530 unfolds. I hope you'll find this concertina-fold book as exciting as I do. It has many possibilities beyond sampler stitches.

The last project is another quick gift idea, though you'll want to make thoughtful pillowcases for your own use, too. I used the alphabet on my Bernina and programmed words into the sewing machine memories, then slipped batting into the pillowcase hems and decorated personal cases and sheets with thoughts.

Look at all of these projects and be creative. Use the techniques in other ways in your home, and try them on wearables, too.

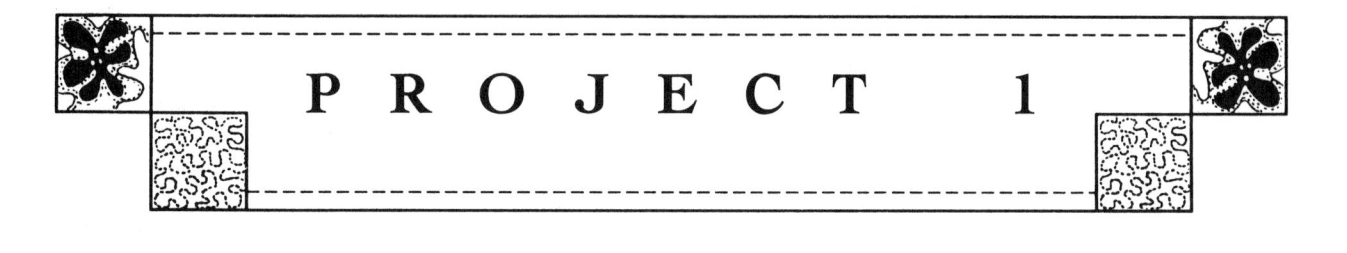
Machine-Quilted Sampler

"Do you machine quilt because it's faster?" is a question I'm often asked. Or someone may volunteer, "Of course you machine quilt because you don't have time for hand quilting." Somehow the idea that I machine quilt because I enjoy it, or because the effects I want can't be accomplished by hand, escapes some people. It's a common belief that the reason one machine quilts is because there's a lack of time, patience, or talent to hand quilt. I hope the projects in this book show you that machine quilting is a tech-

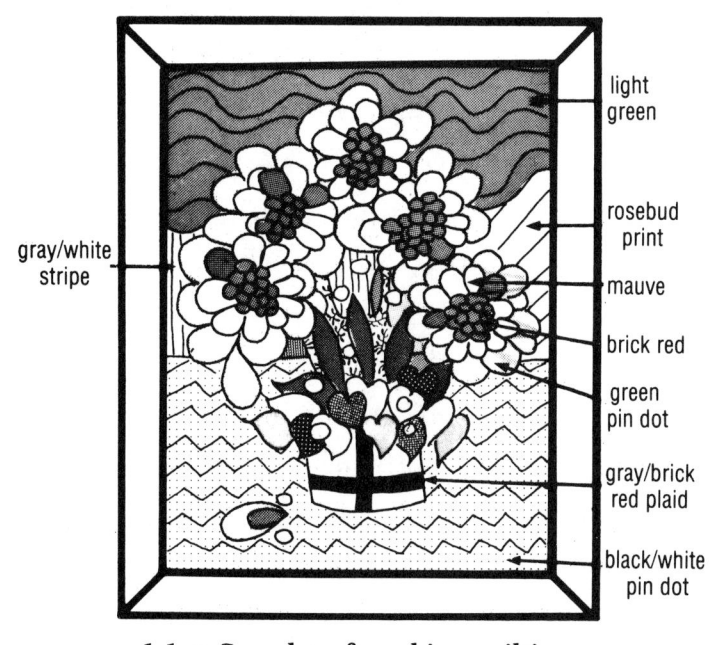

light green

rosebud print

mauve

brick red

green pin dot

gray/brick red plaid

black/white pin dot

gray/white stripe

1.1 ▪ Sampler of machine-quilting.

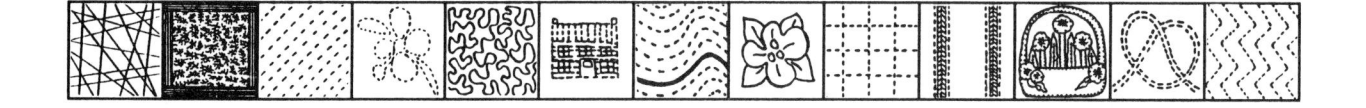

Presser foot: embroidery (20); zigzag (0); zipper (4); darning (9), free-embroidery (24), or quilting (29)

Batting: 1 yard × 1½ yards (.95m × 1.4m) fusible fleece for backing pin dot, stripe, rosebud fabrics, and frame; handful of fiberfill

Miscellaneous: paper-backed fusible web, silver quilt pencil, yardstick, rotary cutter and mat, glue stick, quilting pins, three small plastic rings (optional), 8 yards (7.3m) of ¼" (6mm) cable cord

nique of its own. Yes, machine quilting goes faster, but it isn't a clone of hand quilting. It has its own personality and style, and machine quilters are still experimenting and finding new ways to use it.

All machine quilting is placed in one of two categories: stitching with feed dogs raised, or stitching with feed dogs lowered or covered.

Included in the first category (feed dogs raised) is stitch-in-the-ditch, trapunto, Italian cording, sashiko, echoing, and stitching with decorative or straight stitches in straight or curved lines (Figs. 1.2-1.7). The second category, called free-machine quilting, is

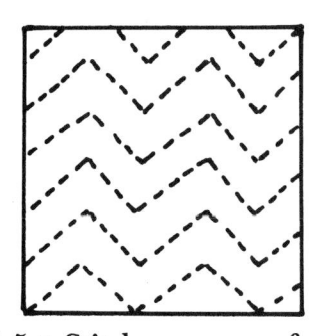

1.2 ▪ Stitch-in-the-ditch on top of a seam.

1.3 ▪ Pad area between quilting stitches to raise an area (trapunto).

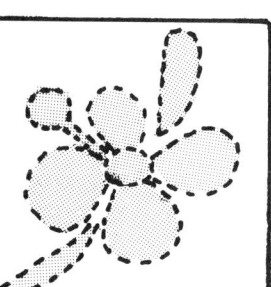

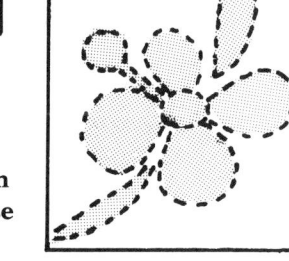

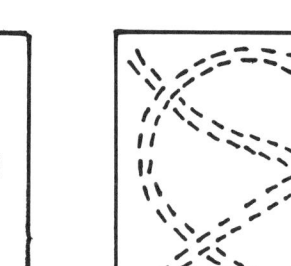

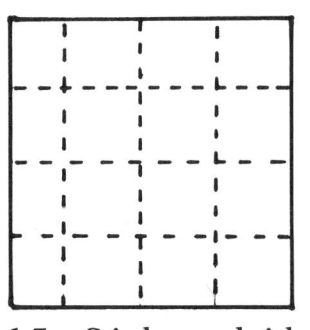

1.4 ▪ Thread cord through a channel between a double row of stitches (Italian cording).

1.5 ▪ Stitch even rows of quilting for one type of sashiko (simple running stitches to hold layers of fabric together).

1.6 ▪ Embellish printed fabric with straight or decorative machine stitches.

1.7 ▪ Stitch a sandwich of fabric and batting together with sewing-machine quilting.

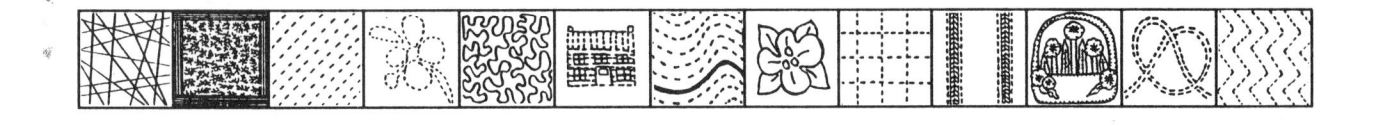

accomplished with the feed dogs lowered or covered. It includes stippling, outlining, drawing, echoing, and trapunto.

In the flowered wallhanging are examples of most of these techniques.

It doesn't look "quick" to you? Read through the directions first to discover how fast this can be sewn. I constructed the large hanging in three smaller sections, which I sewed together later. It's easier to work on smaller sections so it takes less time. Also, if a section has to be replaced because I've made a mistake too awful to rip out or cover up, it's far easier to replace a small section than it is the entire hanging. You'll discover, too, that exact patterns aren't used. Though I give you an idea of a shape, they are all cut out freehand.

Although I used a traditional satin stitch to appliqué parts of the hanging, most of the pieces in the bouquet of flowers are held in place by stretching black bridal veil (tulle) over the batting-backed picture. The petals and leaves are trapped between veil and background by stitching around them. What an easy, fast way to appliqué and quilt at the same time.

Except for this wallhanging, I use the same color scheme on all the projects in this chapter. The colors include pink, mauve, blue, peach, yellow, green, ivory and white. Prints, stripes, checks, pindots, and plain fabrics are used.

The finished picture, without frame, is 30" × 22½" (76cm x 57cm). It has an added, mitered border (4½" [11.5cm]) around it.

1.8 ▪ Stippling, quilting with feed dogs lowered, looks like jigsaw-puzzle cuts.

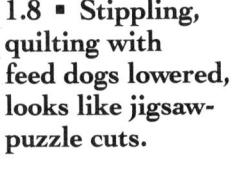

1.9 ▪ Free-quilting is effective when outlining designs in fabrics.

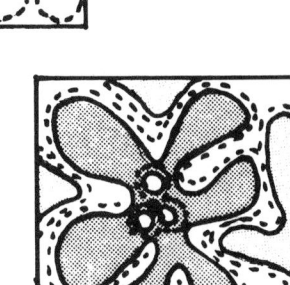

1.10 ▪ Quilt in your own designs.

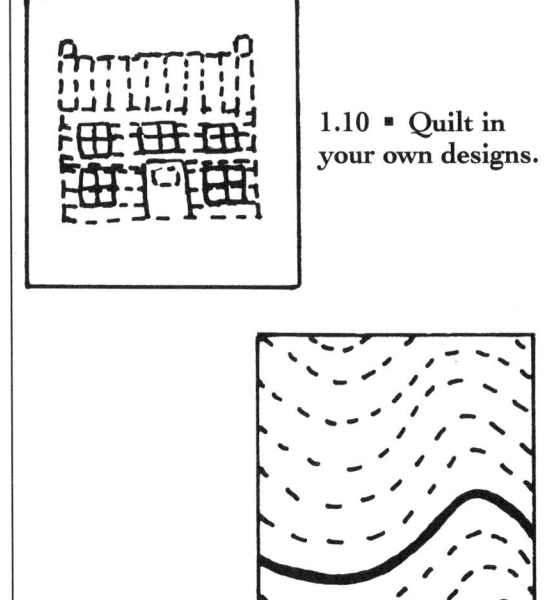

1.11 ▪ Echo quilting a line in a design.

1.12 ▪ **Quilt striped fabric with both straight stitching and decorative machine-stitches.**

1.13 ▪ **Use lines of diagonal stitches to quilt the rosebud fabric.**

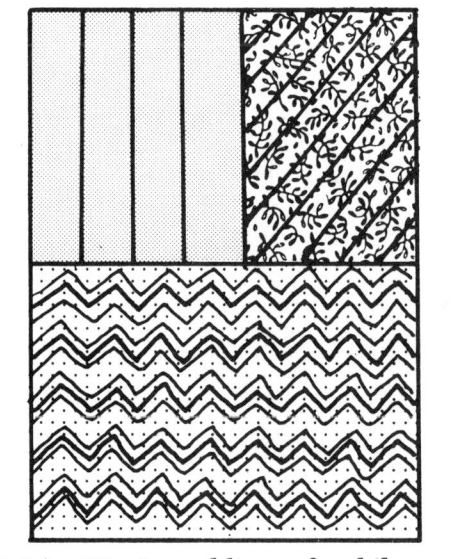

1.14 ▪ **Use jagged lines of sashiko at the bottom of the wallhanging.**

Back the piece of gray/white striped chintz with fusible fleece. Fusible fleece is a 100 percent polyester, needle-punched fleece with a fusible backing (it eliminates basting and saves time). Use rose rayon thread and quilt lines of decorative stitches between stripes, and lines of straight stitches at the sides of some stripes. Put this aside.

Place the rosebud print on the table and draw diagonal lines (a yardstick apart) with a silver quilting pencil. Cover all the fabric with these lines. Back with fusible fleece, then straight-stitch on the marked lines, using black thread.

Draw zigzag lines on the pin dot fabric. These are approximately 1½″ (4cm) long on the diagonal and 1¾″ (4.5cm) high. After backing the fabric with fusible fleece, stitch in a zigzag design like sashiko. With black in the bobbin, to match the fabric, the needle threaded with doubled rose, rayon machine-embroidery thread or smoke monofilament thread, stitch the jagged lines with stitch length slightly longer than normal (stitch length 3). (I varied the thread color by stitching two lines with monofilament, then one row with rose thread. I followed this progression from the top to the bottom of the pin dot.) Unlike a perfect sashiko, I skipped a line or two for variety.

Assemble the three parts of the picture you have finished. To do this, fold under the righthand side of the striped fabric and overlap the rosebud fabric. Sew beside the fold with a narrow blanket stitch, letting the short bite catch the fold as you progress.

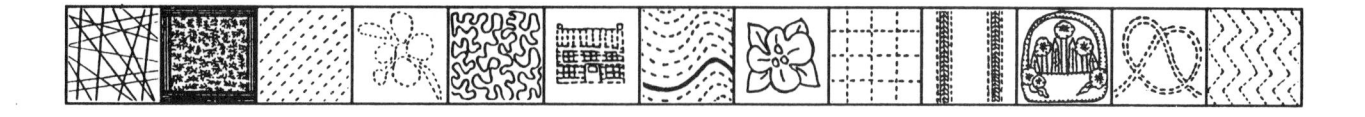

Finish assembling the background by folding under the top of the pin dot fabric, placing it over the edge of the top fabrics, then stitching this in place with the same blanket stitch as before. All the stitching is practically invisible when accomplished with monofilament thread.

Back the light green fabric with fusible fleece and press. Cut the bottom edge in a free-form curving line. Place the fabric over the top 11″ (28cm) of the picture. Straight stitch, with green cotton machine-embroidery thread, along the wavy edge. After smoothing out the fabrics, continue stitching the top of the picture in quilt lines spaced from approximately ½″ (1.3cm) to 1½″ (4cm) apart, echoing the first curved line. Satin stitch (stitch width 3) over the straight stitches at the curved bottom edge.

Fold under ¼″ (6mm) of the sides and bottom edges of the plaid vase, after adding a brick red strip of fabric across it (to visually add weight; see Fig. 1.2). Use rose satin stitches across the top and bottom edges of the strip.

Appliqué the vase to the sashiko piece as shown. Use a wide (3) blanket stitch and black thread for a hand-appliquéd look.

Back several colors of plain green and green print with fusible web. No pattern is needed to cut out four 9″ × 1″ (23cm x 2.5cm) leaves and four ½″ (1.3cm) stems the same length.

Cut out an 8″ (20.5cm) square of green print fabric and back it with fusible web. Then cut out a multi-stemmed design, place

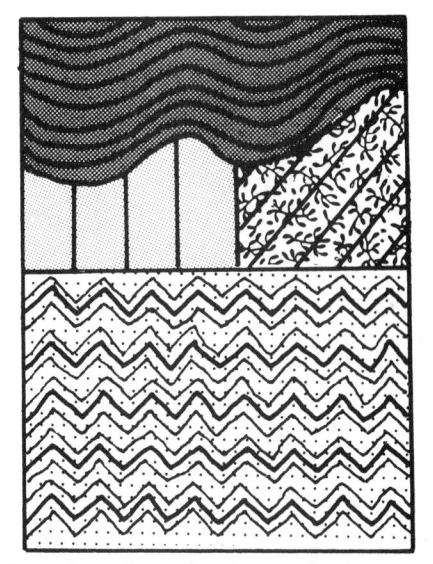

1.15 ▪ Attach and echo-quilt the top area.

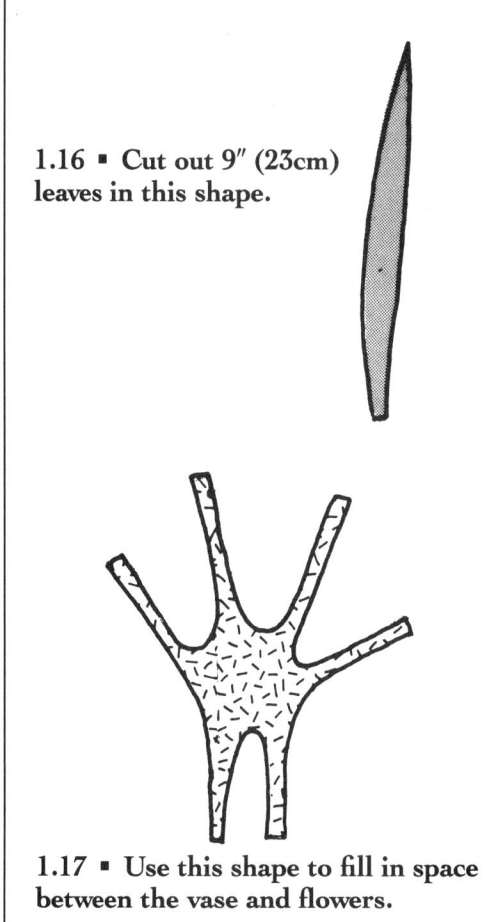

1.16 ▪ Cut out 9″ (23cm) leaves in this shape.

1.17 ▪ Use this shape to fill in space between the vase and flowers.

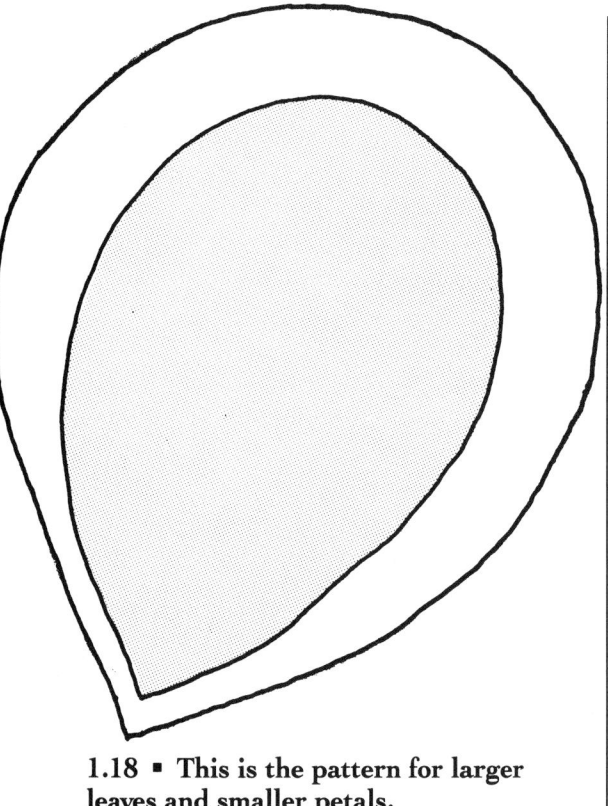

1.18 ▪ **This is the pattern for larger leaves and smaller petals.**

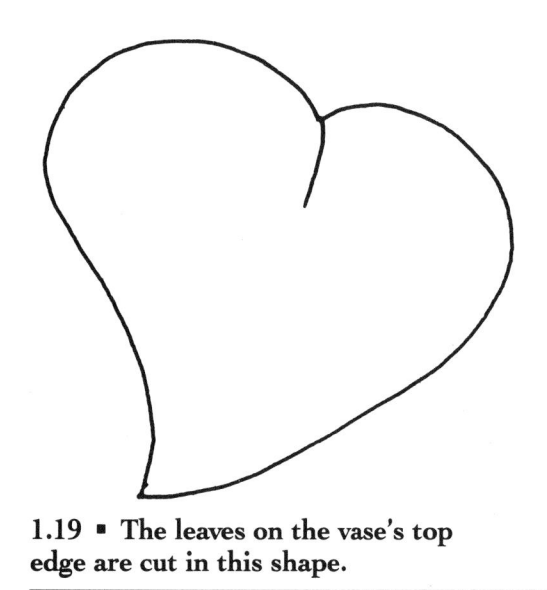

1.19 ▪ **The leaves on the vase's top edge are cut in this shape.**

it over the background on top of the vase, and press in place. Satin stitch (stitch width 2) with green thread at the edges.

Arrange the four long stems and the long leaves over the print piece and press in place.

Prepare the flowers next. Cut out all the petals from brick-colored chintz first (you will need approximately sixty petals). Cut seven to eight mauve petals for variety.

Cut 5 backing circles (1¾″ [4.5cm]) from any scrap fabric and arrange approximately 10 to 12 petals around on top of each circle, adding one or 2 mauve petals to each flower. Use a glue stick to hold them in place on the backing. When finished, cut flower centers from the flowered fabric, or use a fabric of your own choice. Glue that on top of the petals in the center.

Arrange the flowers over the stems and leaves on the wallhanging. Before attaching them, cut out approximately 36 green leaves from green pin dot fabric (see Fig. 1.18). These are slightly larger, but the same tear-drop shape as the flower petals. Slip these leaves behind and around the flowers. Add a tiny bit of fiberfill behind some of the petals and flower centers to give a trapunto look to the flowers when quilting is completed. Use a glue stick sparingly to hold the leaves and flowers in place.

Now cut out leaves for the top of the vase. Use plain fabrics or those cut from the flowered fabric (cut freely, but use this irregular heart shape for all sizes). Arrange them and glue in place with glue stick.

Place a leaf and one petal next to the vase

on the pin dot tablecloth as if they've fallen off. Cut out about a dozen tiny ½" (1.3cm) circles from a yellow/green fabric. Sprinkle those over the stems and leaves.

Cover the picture with black tulle and pin it in place to hold all the small pieces while stitching.

Prepare the machine for free quilting by lowering or covering the feed dogs and placing a free-machine, quilting, or darning foot on the machine. Use smoke monofilament thread to stitch around the petals and into the flower centers. Stipple the centers (see Fig. 1.18). Continue quilting outside the edges of the leaves and stems; then stitch around the outside of the leaves on top of the vase. Use your imagination as you finish quilting wherever it's needed.

If you find areas that need more batting, slit the backing of the wallhanging and slip fiberfill inside.

Change the machine to regular sewing and stitch around the outside of the picture to keep the tulle in place.

To make the frame around the collage, cut the striped fabric (1⅓ yard [1.2m] length) into four lengths, each 5" (12.5cm) wide. Back the strips with fusible fleece (don't press yet). Stitch ¼" (6m) from the edge of the strips, then slip a piece of cording inside the batting against the stitches and use a zipper foot to stitch on the other side of the cord to hold it in place. Trim batting from the seam allowance. Press the frames to fuse batting in place, but leave 1" (2.5cm) unpressed along the edges. Now add other

1.20 ▪ Stitch around the outside of the petals and into the center to stipple the middle area.

1.21 ▪ Free-quilt around the outside edges of all the leaves: behind the flowers, at the top of the vase, and between the long leaves and stems.

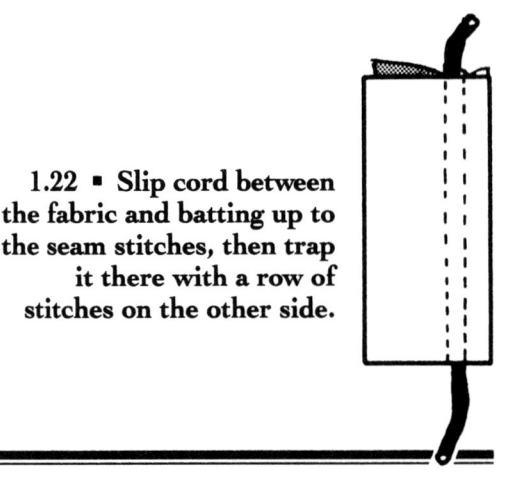

1.22 ▪ Slip cord between the fabric and batting up to the seam stitches, then trap it there with a row of stitches on the other side.

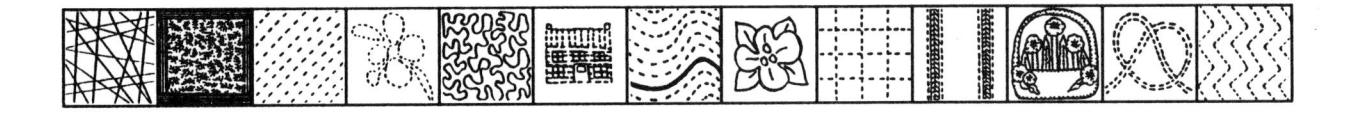

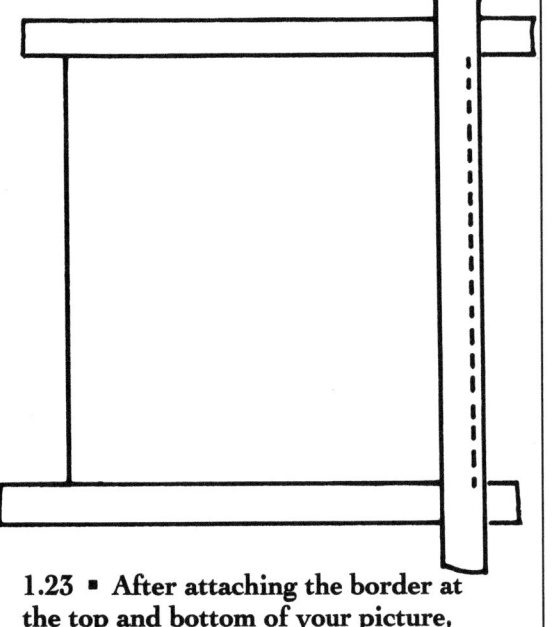

1.23 ▪ **After attaching the border at the top and bottom of your picture, attach the sides. Stitch from top to bottom of the collage, stopping at the inner edge.**

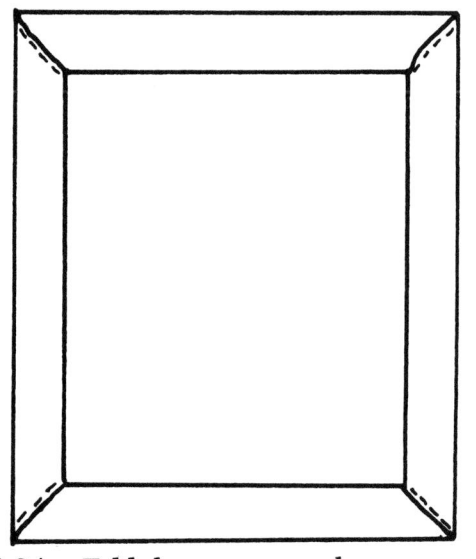

1.24 ▪ **Fold the corners on the diagonal at each corner; baste, then machine-stitch in place.**

quilting lines down the length of the strip to hold the fleece and frame together, leaving ¾" (2cm) open at the edge. Slip cording in between batting and fabric and pull the top fabric around the cord and to the back of the frame. Pin, then use a zipper foot to stitch close to the side of the cable cord.

Next, attach the frame, cut edge nearest center panel. Center and sew on top and bottom strips first (don't trim back yet). Then pin frames to the sides of the picture, extending them beyond the collage and cutting each side to align with the top and bottom. Go back and stitch the sides to attach them, stopping at the top of the inner edge. Then fold the frame under diagonally on each side, top and bottom, to miter the corners. Baste this by hand, but finish by machine stitching on the diagonal fold line. Trim.

Place the picture right side down on a flat surface and measure for the backing. Then measure the black chintz backing to fit, adding a ½" (1.3cm) seam allowance all around it. Cut it out, then stitch around the backing on the seam allowance for ease in folding under. Fold under on the stitched lines and press. Place the backing over the picture and pin, then hand stitch to attach it.

Stitch small plastic rings on the back at each side and center for hanging, or make a casing and hand stitch it to the top back for a dowel hanger.

Appliquéd Wall Hanging

This is my favorite way to appliqué. Not only is there a design of fabric on fabric, but the lines of stitches create a second design. While appliquéing, I quilted at the same time.

For each square, place a piece of plain fabric over a square of flannel. Over that arrange scraps of colors to your liking, including a large circle or large and smaller circles—each square is different. Don't worry about raw edges on the scraps.

Next, place a piece of pink tulle over the scraps. Pin in place. Use the shocking pink thread, the zigzag or patchwork foot, and a straight stitch. Push needle-down button on your machine. Start at one side of the square, straight stitching from top to the bottom. When you get to the end, use the

YOU WILL NEED:

Fabric: 15 squares (10″ [25.5cm] each) and scraps of these colors: shocking pink, salmon, cream, yellow, lavender, blue, green, pink; pink tulle to cover squares; flannel backing for each square; 15 large (3½″ [9cm] diameter) circles in shocking pink or lavender; 15 smaller (2″ [5cm] diameter) circles in other colors; 1½ yards (1.4m) of deep lavender cotton for lattice and binding; 1½ yards (1.4m) of lavender-and-white check glazed cotton for backing

Needle: #90/14 or topstitch, hand-sewing

Thread: rayon variegated (pink, green, yellow, blue) machine-embroidery thread (Natesh #1511); shocking pink rayon machine embroidery thread, sewing, clear monofilament

Presser foot: zigzag (0) or patchwork (37), free-embroidery (24) (optional)

Miscellaneous: rotary cutter and mat; 6″ × 24″ (15cm x 61cm) clear plastic ruler; 5″ × 44″ (13cm × 1.1m) thin bonded batting for binding (cut into five long 1″ [2.5cm] strips), glue stick, water-soluble marker; dowel, plastic rings, or Velcro for hanging.

1.25 ▪ Appliquéd Wall Hanging.

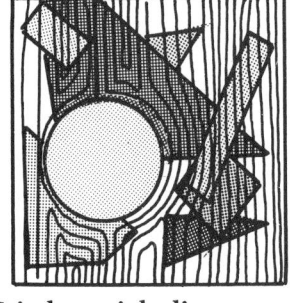

1.26 ▪ **Stitch straight lines to attach appliqués and tulle, leaving circles until later.**

1.27 ▪ **Stitch circles beginning at the edge, then traveling around it in ever smaller circles to the center.**

knee lift to raise the presser foot. Turn the fabric, then nudge the foot pedal to raise the needle. Drop the knee lift so the presser foot is back on the fabric a presser foot width away from the first line. Continue stitching to the end of the line.

Continue on in the same manner until you reach a circle. Stitch around the outside of it as shown (each square is stitched differently at your discretion).

When you finish a square, go back to the circles and stitch around and around the circle, gradually reaching the center, and anchor the thread. Use either a free-machine method of stitching or continue stitching with the zigzag foot and straight stitch.

When you finish stitching the squares with shocking pink, go back and, using variegated thread, stitch between each line of stitches already in your square. If a line is closer or farther away than others you've stitched in, don't despair—perfection isn't mandatory.

When you finish, trim the squares to 10″ (25cm) square (with the rotary cutter and mat and your clear plastic ruler). Take the squares back to the sewing machine and stitch around each square a presser foot width from the edge to hold the tulle in place when you start assembling the hanging.

Prepare the lattice next by cutting the lavender fabric into two 2″ × 54″ (5cm × 1.4m) strips. Prepare the binding by cutting two 6″ × 32″ (15cm × 81.5cm) strips for bindings at the top and bottom, and two 2″ × 54″ (5cm × 1.4m) strips for the sides.

Before sewing the wallhanging together,

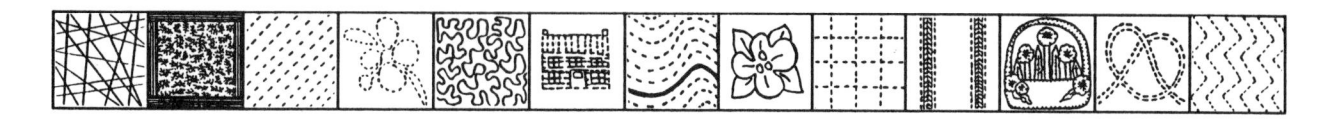

lay out the squares on the floor and arrange them in three rows of five squares each. Check the colors, balance, and stitch direction. It's more interesting if, for example, the stitching on the first square in the first row travels vertically, the one under it travels horizontally, then the third one is vertical again, and so on. On the second row, place the first square horizontal, the second vertical and so on until you have five squares in a row. Lay out the third row of squares the same as the first.

When the arrangement is to your liking, use a water-soluble marker to mark the top back edge of each square. The first number is the row—1, 2, or 3—and the second number is the placement in the row—1, 2, 3, 4, or 5 (so the first square in the first row is numbered 1-1). I can't stress this system enough. Even though you are sure you won't goof up the squares' placement, or the edges to attach, it does happen.

Now stitch the lattice under 1-1 (use ½″ [13mm] seam allowance), cut off the lattice at the end, and stitch on square 1-2. Use the cut-off strip of lattice and stitch at the bottom of that square. Add the next square (1-3) and the lattice at the bottom. Continue adding squares and lattice for each of the three rows, always starting and ending with squares. Then sew the rows together with lattice between those, too. Add 2″-wide (5cm) binding at each side. Press the seams to one side (they have minds of their own, so don't fight them).

Measure the wallhanging before you cut out

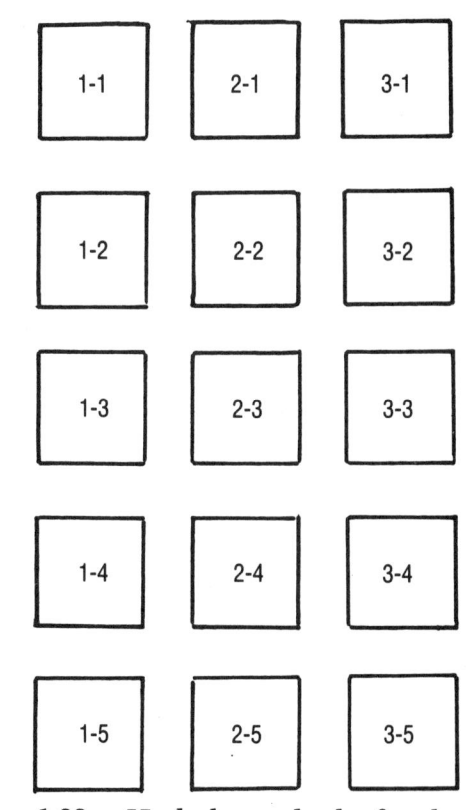

1.28 ▪ **Mark the top back of each square to indicate placement.**

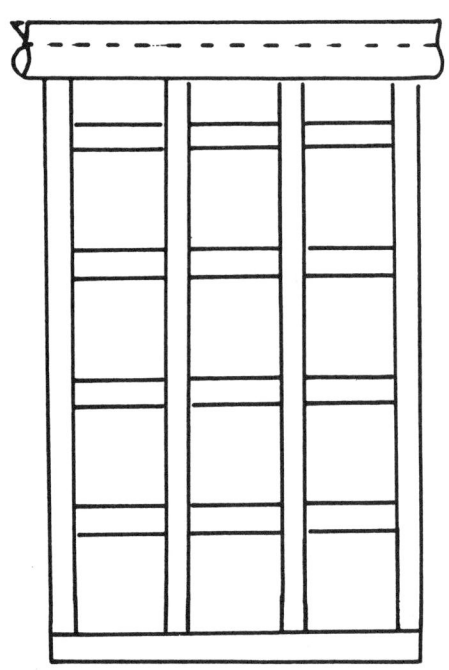

1.29 ▪ **Fold binding strip in half the long way and sew to the front of the wallhanging.**

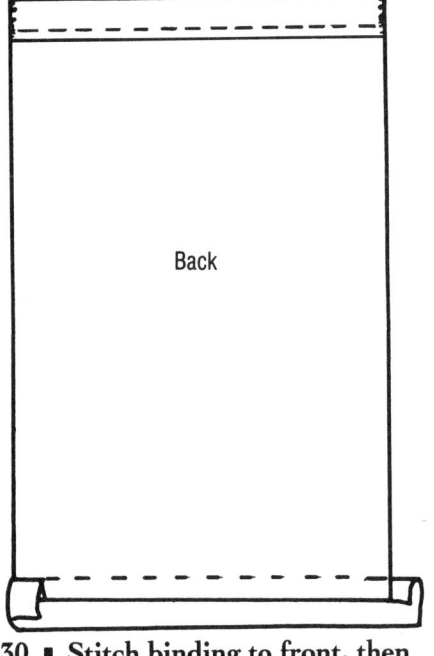

Back

1.30 ▪ **Stitch binding to front, then pull under to the back past the seam, and stitch-in-the-ditch from the front. Hand-stitch edges closed.**

and attach the backing. Trim the backing if necessary. I used checked fabric because it is so easy to sew a straight line with the checks as a guide. Stripes would work just as well.

Place top and backing right sides together and stitch down each side. Place dots of glue stick the length of the side lavender binding. Then put a strip of batting in place on each side (the batting is pieced by butting together).

Turn this giant tube right side out. Stitch-in-the-ditch at each side of the binding (it holds the batting and backing in place).

Finish attaching the binding by folding and pressing one 6″ (15cm)-strip the long way, wrong sides together. Place the cut edges on the top edge of the wallhanging, letting it extend at least ½″ (13mm) beyond the hanging at both ends. Neaten the edges.

Place a strip of batting to the right of the stitching line before you pull the folded edge around and under to the back and slightly past the stitched line. Fold under the fabric extensions at the four corners. Glue sparingly to hold the corners and the binding in place while you stitch-in-the-ditch from the front and catch the binding in your stitches underneath. Use a hand-sewing needle to whip stitch the ends closed.

Sew on a fabric sleeve for a dowel, or several plastic rings to hang it. Or nail a wood lath to the wall, the same width, or slightly shorter, than the wallhanging. Glue a strip of Velcro to it. Attach the other side of the Velcro strip to the back of the wallhanging. The wallhanging then hangs evenly, and is easily removed.

Flower Garden Pillows

Sometimes ideas grow out of necessity, as this one did. Years ago my mother gave my daughter a quilt made by a third relative named Catherine—like the two of them. A pastel Grandmother's Flower Garden, it was an array of 1930s fabrics, an assumption that was confirmed by the embroidered date found under Catherine's name in the corner. Our Cathy used the quilt as a bedspread because I insisted on it. I didn't want it folded up and put on a shelf, never to be appreciated. I carefully washed it, when needed, and enjoyed seeing it used every day.

YOU WILL NEED:

Fabric: damaged quilt square (14″ [35.6cm]) or substitute a piece of quilted print fabric; coordinating fabric for backing (14″ × 16″ [35.6cm x 40.6cm]); fabric strip for ruffle (5″ × 4⅔ yards [13cm × 4.3m])

Needle: #80/12; #90/14 topstitching

Thread: coordinating sewing, clear monofilament, pastel rayon machine-embroidery threads; variegated rayon (Natesh #1511)

Presser foot: zigzag (0); open machine embroidery (20); embroidery (6); zipper (4); button sew-on (18)

Miscellaneous: Pellon fleece (14″ × 16″ [35.6cm x 40.6cm]); satin picot edge ribbon (¼″ × 1 yard [6.4cm × 9.1m]); embroidered ribbon (1″ × 16″ [2.5cm × 40.6cm]); lace insertion (1″ × 1 yard [2.5cm × 9.1m]); lace scraps, bridal tulle to cover pillow, several yards of fine silky cord, four or five lace motifs, several sizes of pearl buttons, beads (optional); gimp, disappearing marker, rotary cutter and mat, 6″ × 24″ (15cm × 61cm) clear plastic ruler, 16″ (40.6cm) snap tape; 14″ (35.6cm) pillow form

1.31 ▪ **Sketch the front of the Victorian pillow after arranging embellishments.**

Now she has little girls of her own, and the quilt has been used to cuddle up with when sick or on nippy Chicago evenings. It's a member of the family! Our problem is, this family member has suddenly become frayed around the scalloped edges. What is in that orange dye? Each tiny orange hexagon has mysteriously disappeared. On closer scrutiny, there are other hexagons that look downright shredded.

Cathy and I spent several days looking at and considering the future of Catherine's quilt. Our decision? To use it as a background for two pillows (we found the best 14″ [35.5cm] sections and cut them out). Then I covered the squares with cords, ribbons, threads, and lace, with pink bridal tulle over it all to hold everything in place while I embroidered the top with decorative stitches. Over that I sewed down beads and buttons to add to the "more is more" Victorian effect.

By adding all of these embellishments over the quilt square, I covered the damaged areas and kept the shreds from further disintegration—or at least now they'll be trapped behind the tulle.

The fun begins. Bring out all the decorative ribbons, lace, beads, cords, and buttons you may need. Find the damaged areas on the quilt piece and begin decorating by covering those areas first with lace and ribbon. Arrange everything on the pillow, placing even the buttons and beads where you want them. Imagine which decorative stitches you'll use. I sometimes draw in lines for

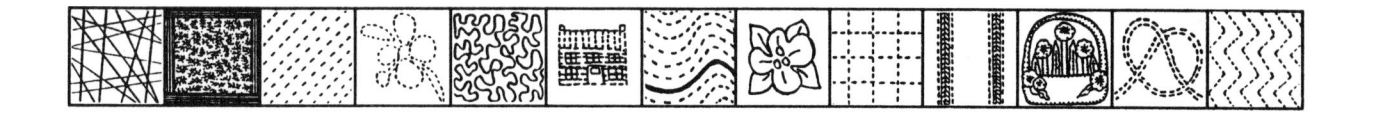

embroidering if I want a certain curve or to cover an area that needs "darning."

I may sketch the arrangement, or sometimes I take a Polaroid picture so I have a plan to follow when I replace the layers.

Once you're pleased with the arrangement, take off the top layers and leave only what you'll place under the tulle. Stitch ribbons and lace in place first with clear monofilament thread. Place pastel pink bridal tulle over the top, then smooth and pin down the edges. Tulle is magical. It's almost invisible and it not only holds little scraps of fabrics, ribbons, and laces in place while embroidering, but it takes the place of heavy stitches around appliqués.

Use free-machine or standard machine stitches and pastel rayon machine-embroidery thread over the tulle to hold it down and decorate. Here are the stitches (found on my 1530 machine) that I chose for the pillows: A1-9, B1-9, F1-2, G1-6, G2-10, H1-4, I2-7, I2-8, I2-9, M1-1, M1-3. Of course you can substitute your favorite stitches found on your own machine. Add stitches at the edges of ribbons, in the centers of ribbons to give them another dimension, or stitched in lines of decorations wherever they add to the look you want to achieve.

Add satin-stitch flowers, made by de-centering the needle to needle left, feed dogs down, open embroidery foot on, needle down, then zigzag stitch (stitch width 3) in one place to build up a flower petal. Ending at needle left, raise the presser foot (remember your knee lifter, which makes this job so

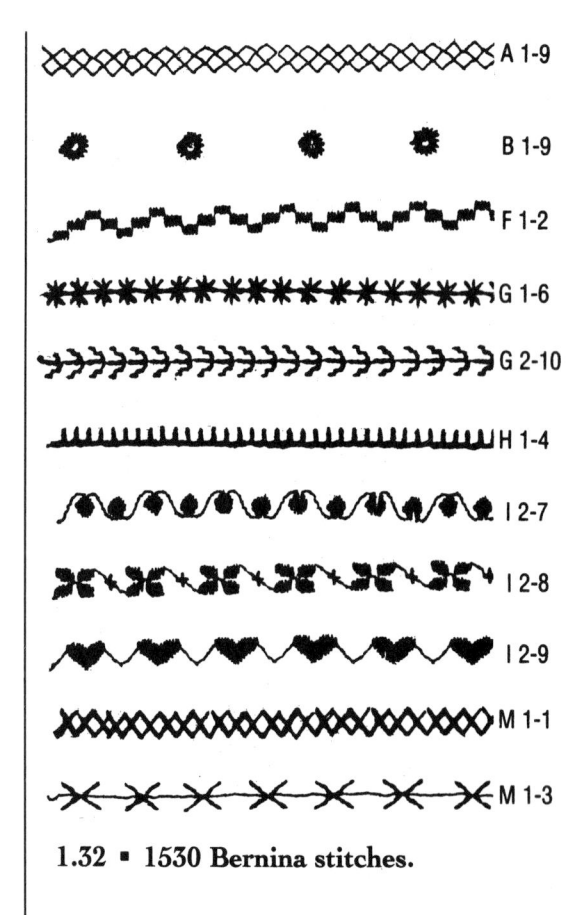

1.32 ▪ 1530 Bernina stitches.

1.33 ▪ Stitch zigzag stitches in place to build up flower petals.

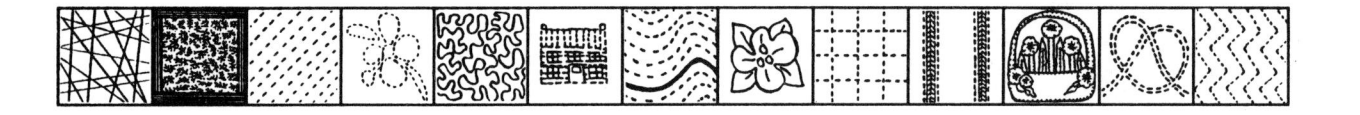

fast), turn the fabric slightly, then stitch again as before to build up another petal of stitches. Proceed around the circle, laying in five or six petals. Scatter these over the pillow top. They're decorative and also help hold the tulle in place.

For the last step, use the fine silky cord to visually hold the buttons together. Place the buttons where you want them, then let the cord drop on top and travel from one button to the next, creating curves and loops between as it travels from one edge of the pillow to the opposite edge. Take the buttons off the top and pin the cord in place. Use the open embroidery foot so you can see what you're doing as you zigzag over the cord with rayon machine embroidery thread. (I used Natesh variegated #1511, which was perfect for my pastel pillow.)

Buttons and beads are last. Sew buttons on by machine, leaving variegated thread in the needle (check your machine's basic manual for directions). Pull thread out of the needle to the start of a color. Stitch a button in place with it. Pull out the thread until you reach another color, and stitch with that color for the second button, and so on, using a different color for each button.

If you are adding beads, be sure the holes are large enough for a machine needle, or string the beads and then couch the whole string of beads down by stitching between them over the thread.

To prepare the backing, cut the fabric into two pieces, 14″ x 8″ (35.6cm × 20cm). Cut the fleece the same size and sew the fleece to

the back of the fabric at the edges (I like the look of batting-backed pillowcases because they look smoother and fill out the pillow better.)

Attach the snap tape on top of the long edge of one of the backing pieces. Check that the snaps are away from the ¼" (6.4mm) seam line. Be sure to check both ends. Pin and then use the zipper foot to stitch down both sides of the tape.

To attach the tape to the other side, first fold under the edge 1" (2.5cm), press and pin. Snap the tape together and place the folded edge over the tape (be sure this side covers the tape and overlaps it slightly). Line up the edges. Pin through from the top to the tape, then unsnap the tape and stitch it to the backing piece from the back side. Once more, snap the tape together. Stitch at each end across the tape at the seam line to make construction easier later. Put this aside.

Piece fabrics if necessary to make the ruffle. Then sew the two short ends right sides together to create a large loop. Press seam open. Fold the loop in half the long way and press wrong sides together. Fold the loop in half crosswise and mark each end with a disappearing marker. Fold again, matching marks, and mark ends again to divide the loop into four sections.

Off the machine, thread gimp through the cording foot (tie an overhand knot behind the foot), then clip the foot on your Bernina and place the foot at the cut edges of the ruffle loop. Using regular sewing thread, zig-

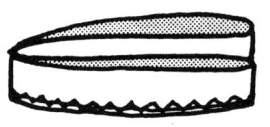

1.34 ▪ **Fold to divide the loop into four sections.**

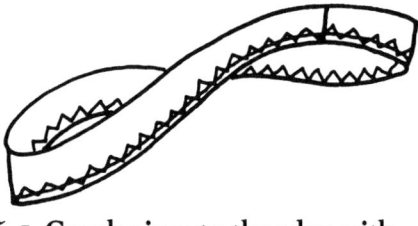

1.35 ▪ **Couch gimp to the edge with zigzag stitches.**

1.36 ▪ **Match the marks on the ruffle and pillow top.**

zag stitch (stitch width 2, stitch length 2), around the loop. The gimp is now covered by zigzag stitches. Put this aside.

Pin the marks on the ruffles to the center of each side of the pillow, cut edges matching. Arrange the ruffles evenly, but pull a bit more fabric into the corners, pin, and stitch the ruffle to the pillow top with a ½″ (13mm) seam allowance. Place the back on top of the ruffles, pin, turn the square over, and stitch from the top around the square on the line of stitching already there. Trim the corners. Open the snap tape, turn the pillowcase right side out, and slip the pillow form inside.

And that is how I gave each of my granddaughters a piece of history that perhaps they can give their own little girls some day.

Sampler of Stitches

The first thing I do when I get a new Bernina is work my way through the basic manual, learning the functions of my new obsession and what the stitches shown in the book look like when actually stitched. Yet it never ends there, because when I want to see what a stitch looks like months later, I either need a reference or I have to stitch off a sample again. So I usually keep all my samples in plastic sleeves in a notebook. But this time I decided to make a book for the 1530.

First you'll make the pages of the book. Then you'll make a separate cover.

Cut white cotton fabric into two pieces: one, 8½" × 54" (1.4m × 21.5cm), the other, 4" × 54" (10cm × 21.5cm). Place the smaller piece of fabric aside; then back the larger piece with tear-away stabilizer.

1.37 ▪ Book of 1530 stitches.

YOU WILL NEED:

Fabric: 12½" × 54" (31.8 × 1.37m) closely woven, blouse-weight white cotton; scraps of fabrics for the cover; 6" × 15" (15cm × 38cm) coordinating fabric for cover lining

Thread: 18 colors rayon or cotton machine-embroidery, white sewing, clear monofilament

Needles: #90/14 sharp (jeans) or topstitching

Presser foot: zig-zag (0), reverse (1), free-hand embroidery (24), walking foot (50), button sew-on (18), open embroidery (20)

Miscellaneous: rotary cutter and mat with grid, 6" × 24" (15cm × 61cm) clear plastic ruler, 13" × 5" (33cm x 13cm) heavy mat board-weight cardboard, glue stick, thick tacky glue, razor cutter (optional), disappearing marker, 8½" × 54" (22cm × 1.37cm) tear-away stabilizer, 3½ yards (3.2m) fine, silky cord, 1 yard (.91m) decorative cord, 6" × 13" (15cm x 33cm) Pellon fleece; 6" × 54" (15cm × 1.37cm) Lite HeatnBond, purchased tassel or make your own, sheet of paper and pencil, spatula or tongue depressor, ¼" (6mm) button

Machine Quilted Sampler adds a splash of color to your decor, while showcasing Bernina stitches and techniques (Project 1).

Above: Appliquéd Wallhanging (Project 2) and the Sampler of Stitches book (Project 4) coordinate well with a soft-toned decor. *Opposite top:* interior of the Sampler of Stitches, a permanent reference to all your favorite Bernina stitches. *Opposite below:* Flower Garden Pillows (Project 3) create a perfect Victorian decorating scheme with beautiful bits of laces and delicate trims.

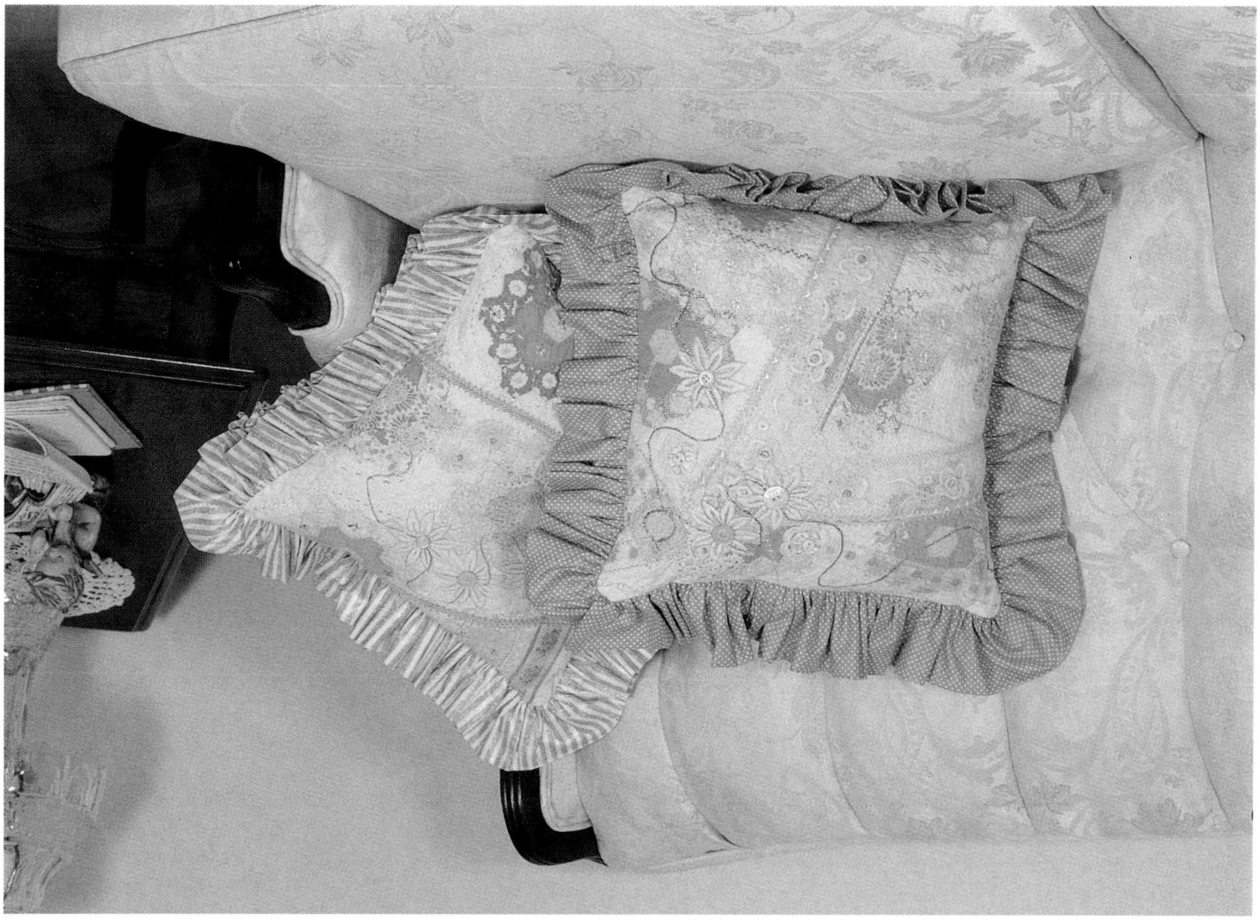

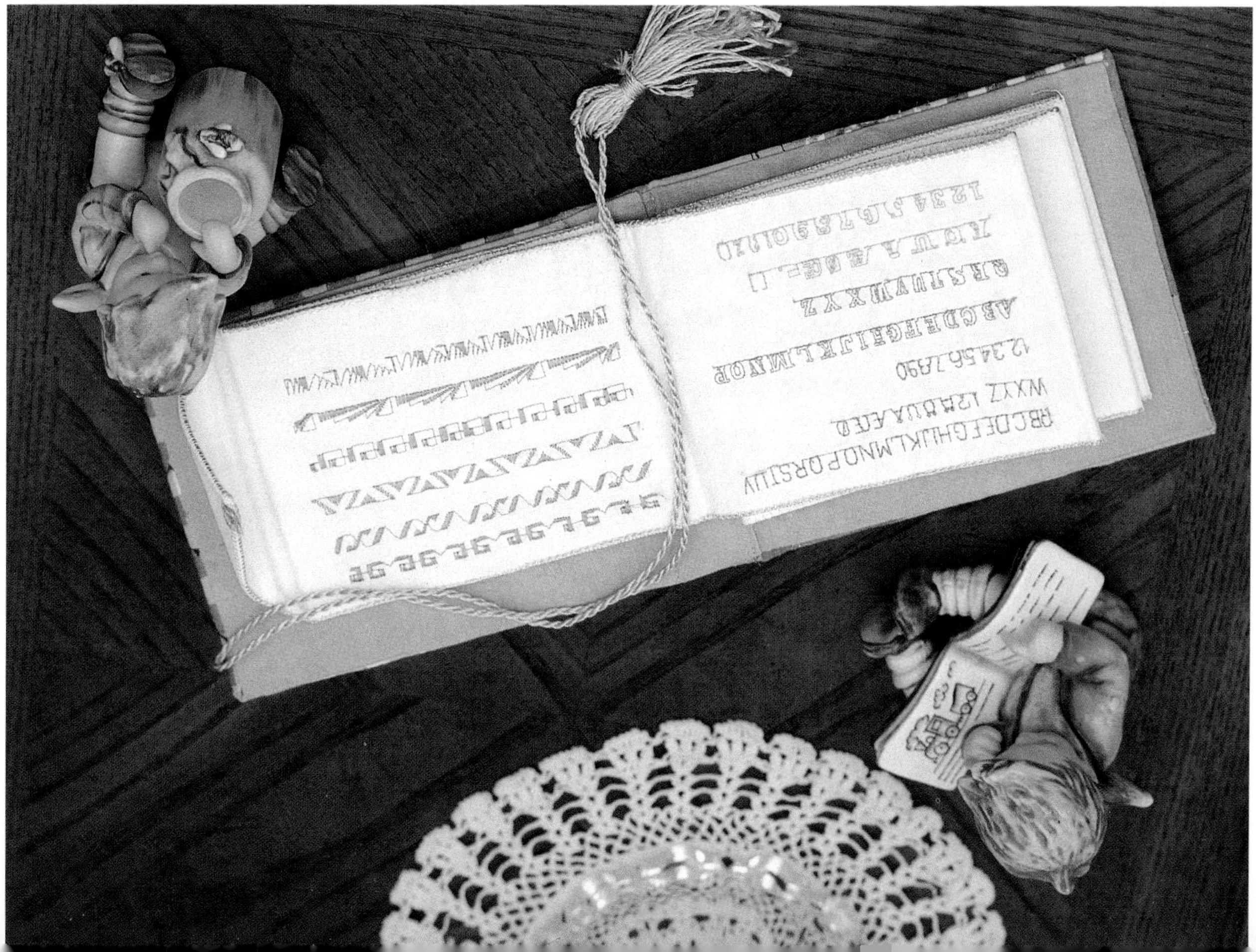

Left: The 90s come alive with brilliant colors when the Duvet Cover/Summer Quilt Combo (Project 13) and Confetti Pillow Sham (Project 14) brighten up a room. *This page, above:* Thoughtful Pillows (Project 5) and Flower Basket Collage (Project 15) add special touches to your own burrow. Personalize them to create imaginative gifts.

Opposite page: Western Wreath, Quilting-the-Print Pillow, and Clipped and Quilted Pillow (Projects 9, 10, and 11) easily extend Southwestern/ Amerindian decor to any room of the house. *This page:* Indian Chief Doll (Project 12) is handsome with any decorating motif, or pair him with Leather Patch Headboard and Leather Appliqué Pillows (Projects 7 and 8) to complete your decorating theme.

The laminated center of the Picnic Mat
(Project 16) makes cleanup a breeze, but won't
keep the ants from sharing your goodies.

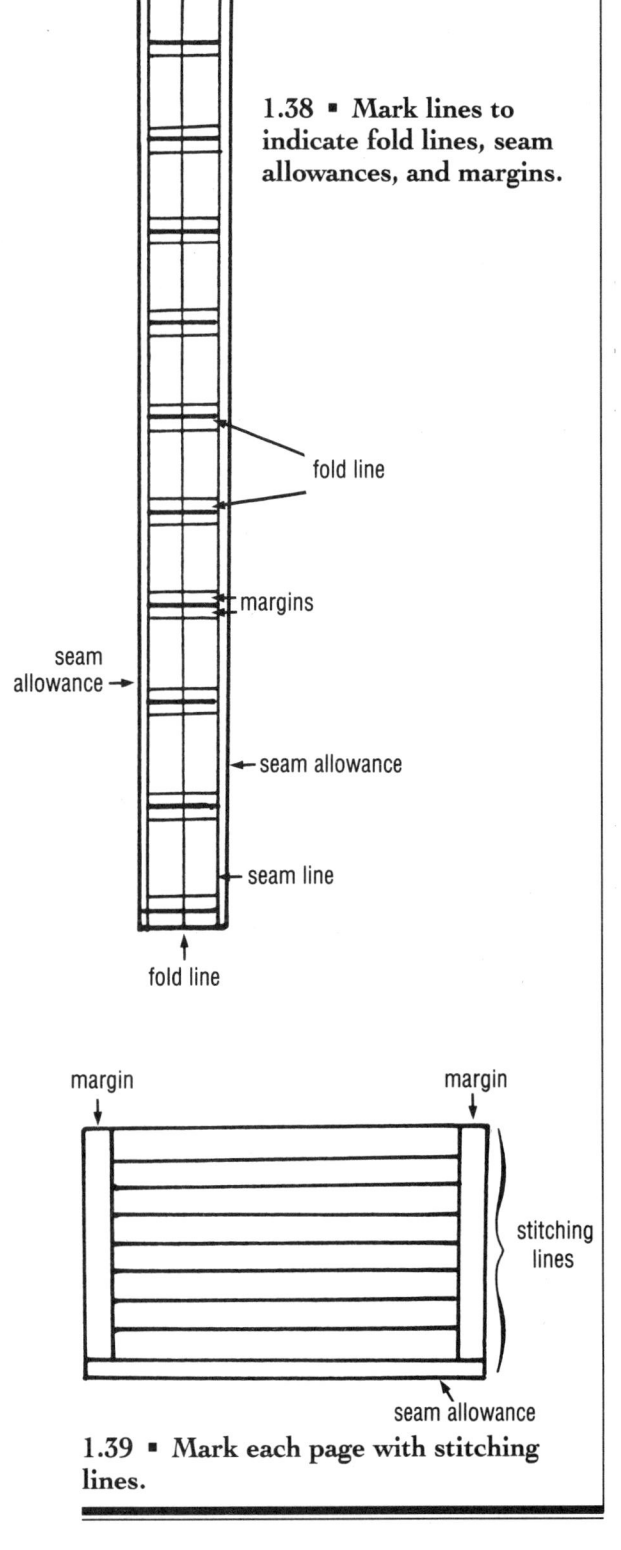

1.38 ▪ Mark lines to indicate fold lines, seam allowances, and margins.

fold line

margins

seam
allowance →

← seam allowance

← seam line

fold line

margin   margin

stitching
lines

seam allowance

1.39 ▪ Mark each page with stitching lines.

Using the mat with a grid printed on it along with the 6″ x 24″ (15cm × 61cm) ruler and disappearing pen, divide the white fabric in half the long way; then mark a line ½″ (13mm) from the lefthand side of the strip on the short end (this line indicates the binding).

From that line to the righthand side, mark a line every 5½″ (14cm) (these are fold lines for the pages). Then turn the strip over and mark the last line (on the righthand side) on the underside of the strip as well. Turn the strip over again to the right side and continue.

The strip is divided into ten sections, but you'll use only nine of them above and below the strip (leave the righthand short section unmarked). As starting and stopping guides when stitching, mark lines ½″ (13mm) on either side of each line you drew except the two end sections (see Fig. 1.39).

Plan the 18 pages by looking through the Bernina basic manual first. Draw seven lines for stitching guides across each page, starting ½″ (13mm) from the top and parallel to the long center line. (There is ¼″ [6mm] seam allowance at the top and bottom of the strip.)

Use a different color thread for each stitch pattern group that shows on the sewing machine screen. If you do, you can find each group later (of course you can indicate the letter and number on each page with a permanent fine-line marker or stitch it in if you wish). Include buttonholes and eyelets, too (don't clip them open), as well as sewn-on

buttons. Center the buttonholes, eyelets, and buttons attractively, ignoring the lines originally drawn in with the disappearing marker.

Stitch the useful stitches first; then add the decorative stitches. You won't have enough space for all of them, but you can solve this problem by dividing some of the lines in half so you do have enough space. I was consistent with one color for one screen even though sewing the stitches on one screen sometimes took two pages.

After all the pages are stitched, carefully remove the tear-away stabilizer. Press fabric to eliminate wrinkles and creases. Fold it in half the long way—with wrong sides together—and press the fold. Put that aside.

Fuse Lite HeatnBond to the smaller strip of white cotton (4" x 54" [10cm × 1.37cm]). Remove the paper backing, then slip it inside the folded strip of stitches and fuse it to one side to stiffen the pages.

To make up the concertina-fold pages, fold the fabric right sides together the long way (but don't press with the iron). Stitch a ¼" (6mm) seam allowance at the bottom. Find the line marked on the underside. Then mark the middle of that line and 2½" (6.5cm) from its center toward the righthand edge. Then draw a line from the top of the fold line to the mark. Draw another line from the bottom of the fold line at the stitched seam to the mark. Stitch on the last two lines, creating a point at the end of the strip. Then stitch three tiny stitches across the point to make turning easier. Trim the fabric from the point and edges; then turn

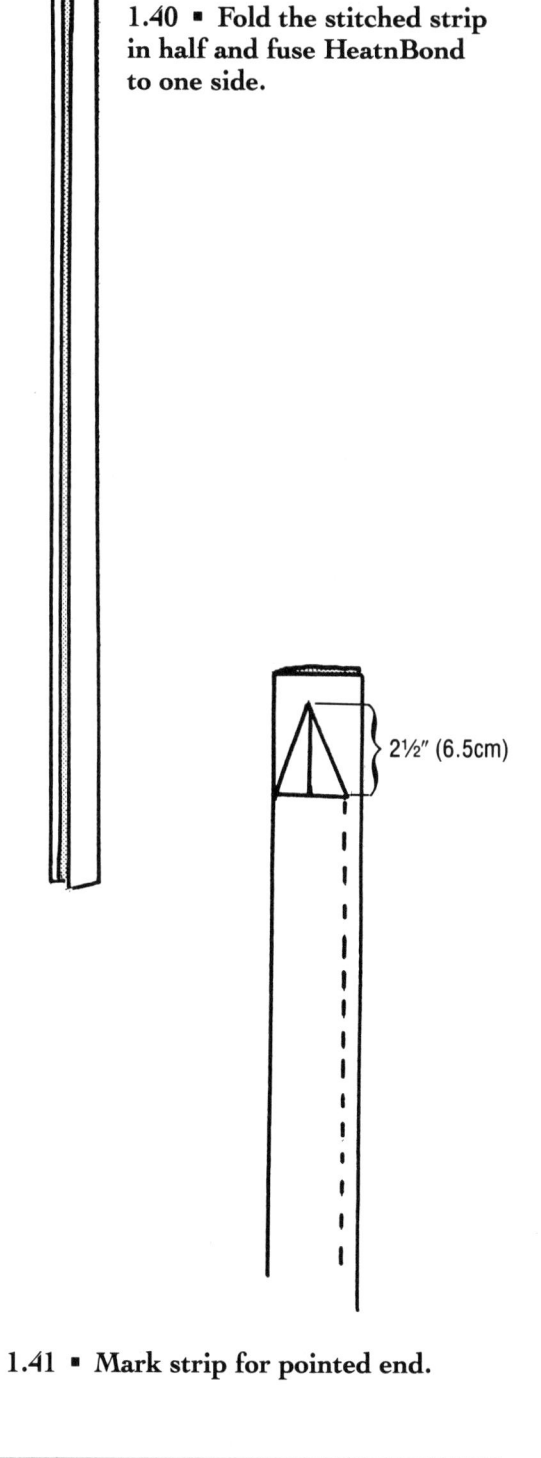

1.40 ▪ **Fold the stitched strip in half and fuse HeatnBond to one side.**

2½" (6.5cm)

1.41 ▪ **Mark strip for pointed end.**

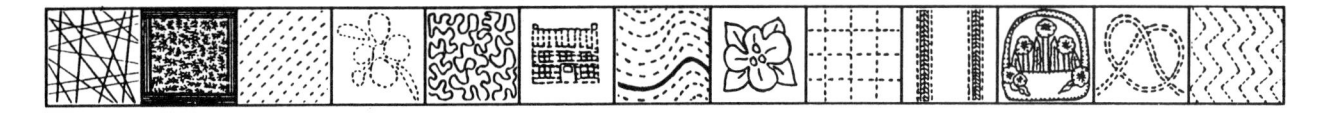

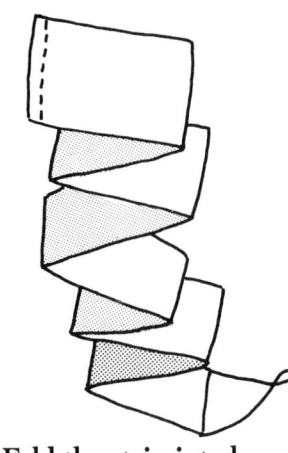

1.42 ▪ Fold the strip into large pleats.

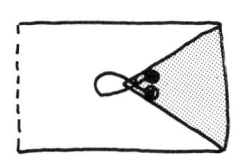

1.43 ▪ Stitch a button loop at the point.

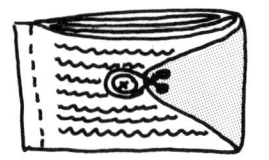

1.44 ▪ Sew a button on the first page of stitches.

the tube right side out and press the seams again to flatten them.

Slip fine, silky cord through the hole in the embroidery foot and tie a knot behind the foot. Place it at the edge of the strip of stitches and zigzag (stitch width 3, stitch length 1½) over the cord, attaching it all around the edge as you do.

Next, stitch down the vertical lines with clear monofilament thread. Then fold the strip concertina-style by folding under the second "page" of the long strip, then folding the third in the opposite direction like giant pleats. Continue folding in pleats and pressing each fold at the same time.

To make the button loop, cut off a small piece of the decorative cord (long enough to slip over the button) and knot both ends separately. Place one end over the other at the knots and straight stitch to the book underneath the pointed end with clear monofilament thread where the loop intersects. Pull the loop back over all the folded pages and find the placement for the button. Mark it, then dot the button with glue stick and place it on the mark. Use the button sew-on foot to stitch the button to the first page with clear monofilament thread. You'll sew the button on top of a line of stitches, but don't despair. There are enough stitches on both sides to identify them.

Be creative with the cover. I pieced it, then machine quilted it in various ways. This is how I did it: First I traced around the cardboard covers on a sheet of paper. Then I divided the outline of the front cover into

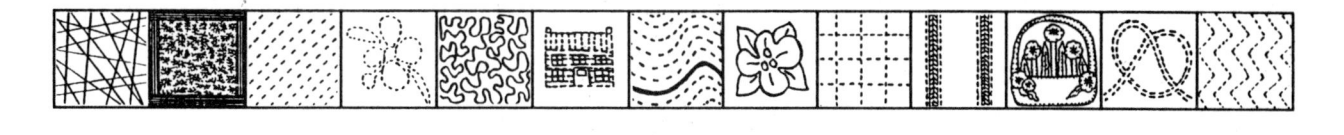

1.45 ▪ **Plan for piecing and quilting the cover.**

sections. In each section I sketched in an example of quilting: sashiko, echoing, trapunto, Italian cording, stippling, quilting with straight and decorative stitches (Fig. 1.3–1.11). Then I cut out and pieced fabric to match the sections I drew, backed the fabric with fleece, and quilted it as drawn on the pattern. I used stitch-in-the-ditch to hold the fleece in place at the *spine* of the pieced cover; then I stippled the spine. The back of the book is one piece of checked fabric. The machine stitches follow the checks of the fabric: vertical lines are straight stitched with rayon thread; horizontal lines are stitched with a decorative machine stitch.

Once the cover is completed, prepare the lining by cutting out one piece of coordinating fabric 6″ × 7″ (15cm × 17.8cm) for the

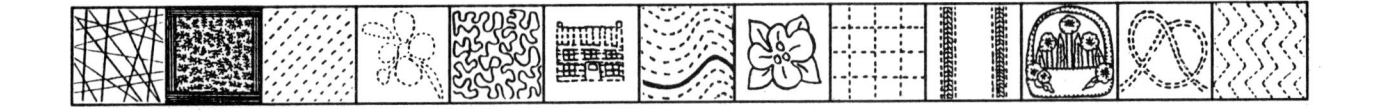

front cover and one piece 6″ × 8″ (15cm × 20.3cm) for the back cover. Stitch around each side of the lining ½″ (13cm) from the edges (the fold line). Fold under at the stitching, and press. Then dot glue stick under the seam allowance to hold it in place; not too much glue—only enough to make the lining easier to work with.

Use either a rotary cutter or razor blade cutter to cut out two pieces of cardboard 5″ × 6″ (13cm × 15cm) for the cover, and a spine 5″ × 1″ (13 cm × 2.5cm).

Assemble the patchwork cover by placing it flat on a table, inside up. On top of it, place the two pieces of cardboard, with the spine between. Leave ⅛″ (3mm) between each piece. Take the cardboard off the cover one piece at a time and, using a spatula or tongue depressor, cover the cardboard pieces with a light coat of thick tacky glue. Then replace them on the fabric cover, glue side down. Run a bead of glue along both long edges of the quilted cover. Pull the long edges over the cardboard and finger press them in place. Glue all along the short edges next but don't pull it over yet. Fold each corner down on an angle and press the fabric together to secure it. Glue again at each end. Pull the sides over the cardboard as before and press in place. Put the cover aside until you finish attaching the page strip and linings.

Place the cut edge of the sampler strip, right sides together, between the unfinished short sides of the two lining pieces. Stitch ½″ (13cm) from the edge.

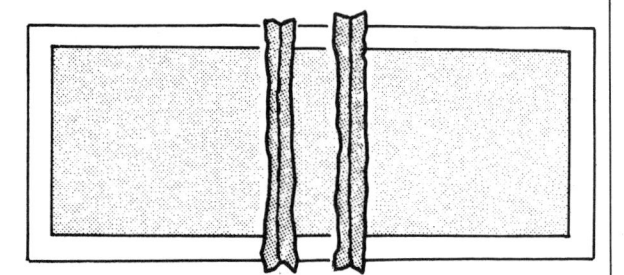

1.46 ▪ **Glue cardboard to the cover.**

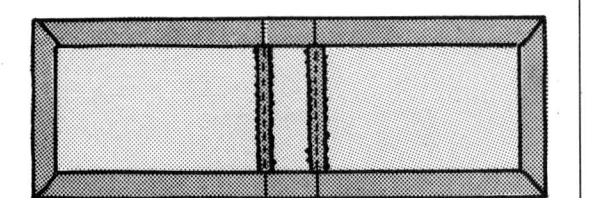

1.47 ▪ **Glue seam allowances to the cover.**

Pin the three layers to the cover at the lefthand side of the spine, seam allowance turned toward the spine (the cover is still open with inside up). Align the seam allowance with the spine. Pin in place or baste by hand for accuracy when stitching the book together later.

Using clear monofilament thread in the bobbin and on top, stitch-in-the-ditch in the seam line between the front cover and the spine. Anchor well at both ends by stitching up and back several times.

Turn the book over so the inside is visible. Pull the back lining over the spine and back cover, matching the edges of the lining to the cover. Pin at both cover corners to hold the fabric taut as you stitch again, stitch-in-the-ditch, from the front through the seam on the other side of the spine and the lining.

Now use thick tacky glue to glue down the folded-under edges of the lining just inside the edges of both cover pieces.

Make or buy a cord and tassel to hold the book together. You'll need at least 32" (81.5cm) of cord. Hold the two ends together and tie thread around them about 3" (7.5 cm) from the end, creating a loop and the start of a tassel. Add more cord inside the loop over the tie to make the tassel plumper. Tie ½" (13cm) from the top of the tassel with a piece of the cord. Trim the tassel ends.

Place the top of the loop on the closed book's bottom front edge. Pull the tassel around the book and through the loop in front to hold the book together.

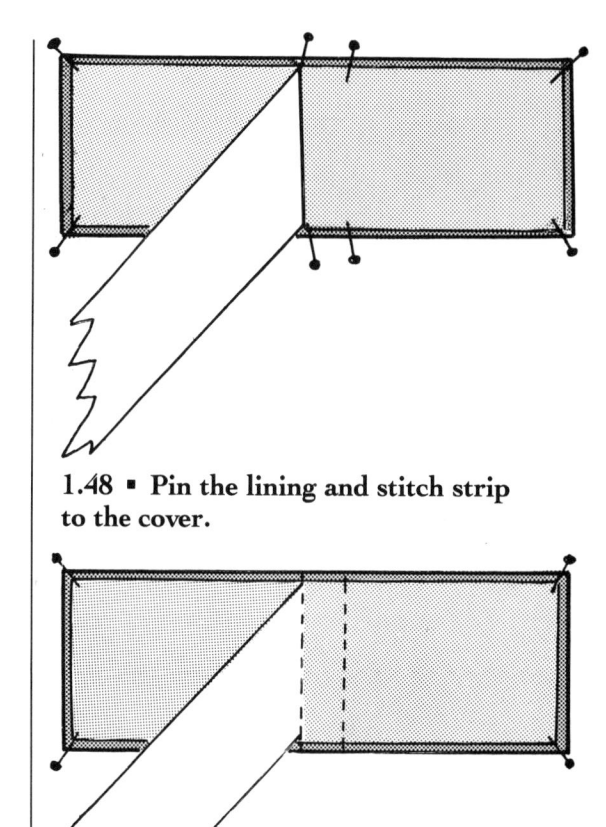

1.48 ▪ **Pin the lining and stitch strip to the cover.**

1.49 ▪ **Stitch-in-the-ditch through the seam and lining to hold it together.**

1.50 ▪ **Pull the tassel around the book and through the loop in front.**

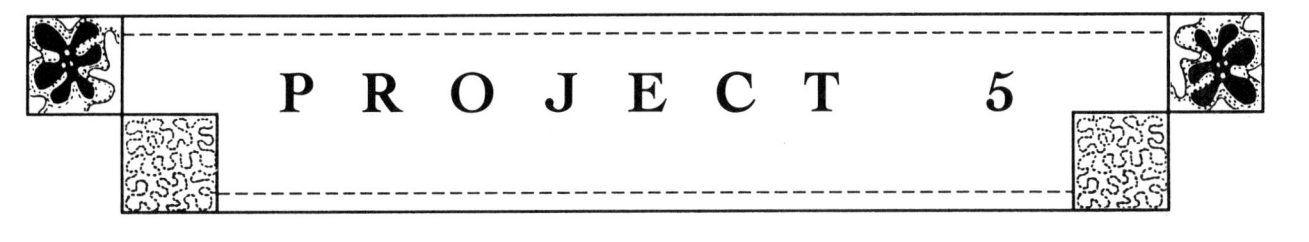

YOU WILL NEED:

Fabric: two pillowcases—your color choice

Needle: #90/14, hand-sewing

Thread: sewing or machine-embroidery thread of your choice; sewing thread—colors of the pillowcases

Presser foot: zigzag (0), reverse (1), or walking foot (50)

Miscellaneous: embroidery scissors, disappearing marker, Pellon fleece or flannel the width and length of pillow hem

Thoughtful Pillowcases

Remember how we all wanted a sewing machine with alphabets and numbers? Then, after acquiring one and making obligatory name tags, we thought to ourselves, if not aloud, "Now what? How will I use alphabets and numbers?" Here is my latest favorite idea to use for any age, any occasion, or any person. If you haven't mastered programming the memory in your machine, you'll learn while doing on this project, and have fun as well.

First of all, I think pillows are as important to kids—if not more important—than their blankets. They carry them to slumber parties, throw them on the floor in front of the TV, and take them to Grandma's for a weekend. Whenever I think of car trips, I visualize our kids lining up at the car door with their pillows. On the pillows were favorite pillowcases—Batman, Mickey Mouse, or those their Grandma made special for them from favorite colors and fabrics.

Although you could make a pillowcase from scratch, I usually embellish ready-mades with monograms and embroidery. These two pillowcases, which I embellished with the Bernina alphabet, are an evolution of those personal pillowcases my daughter

1.51 ▪ Thoughtful pillowcase.

took to slumber parties, the pillows we took on trips, and the ones I've monogrammed and embroidered.

First, open approximately 12″ (30.5 cm) of the pillowcase side seam so it will lay flat for stitching. Also clip out the hem stitches.

Cut a piece of Fleecy Pellon or flannel fabric the size of the hem. Slip it up to the hem's fold and use a few pins to hold it there. To guide your stitching, draw three lines with a disappearing marker, starting 1″ (2.5cm) from the edge of the pillowcase and 1″ (2.5cm) apart.

If you aren't sure how to program the Bernina's memory, get out the basic manual now to guide you through the process—it's extremely easy. When I began planning the first pillowcase, I knew I wanted to write out poetry or quotations using the word *sleep* for inspiration, so I wrote down all the poetry or quotes I could think of that included that word and decided on the following combination for the first pillowcase: "AND MILES TO GO BEFORE I SLEEP"; "THE INNOCENT SLEEP"; "SLEEP THAT KNITS UP THE RAVELLED SLEEVE OF CARE"; "TO SLEEP: PERCHANCE TO DREAM."

To help inspire you, find a book such as *Bartlett's Familiar Quotations* (visit the library for help if necessary). But don't limit yourself to quotes or poetry. What about spelling out a name over and over? Or an evening prayer? There are unlimited options.

When you program your machine, I suggest you put each quote into a separate memory, even though you may have room to

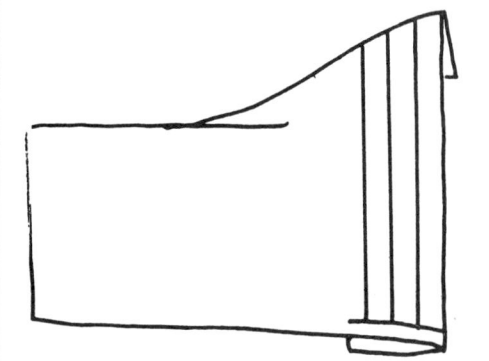

1.52 ▪ Draw three lines across the pillowcase hem as stitching guides.

include more than one in the seventy spaces allotted.

Always stitch a sample first. Slip a piece of flannel between two pieces of pillowcase-like fabric and stitch through the memories to be sure you like the choice of thread and that the bobbin and top tensions are balanced. Don't rule out using regular sewing thread like Metrosene. It wears well—pillowcases are washed and dried a lot—and it also creates a clear-cut letter; I like it. Arrange the letters so the tops of them point toward the body of the pillowcase, not the folded edge. Start in ½" (13mm) from the seam edge, using the drawn line as a guide for your stitches. Run through all the memories you used before starting at the first one again. Leave two or more spaces after each period between quotations. Stitch slowly at the end of the line to complete a whole letter (don't concern yourself with finishing a word or a sentence at the end of a line). Leave long thread ends before clipping them, and start again at the top of the next line, continuing where you left off previously.

When you reach the end of the third line, change thread to the same color as the pillowcase and restitch the top of the hem. Trim back the batting if needed.

Finish by stitching up the seam: first with a straight stitch, then overcast with a zigzag stitch, or serge the edge in one step. Then use a hand-sewing needle to bring the top decorative threads to the back and anchor the bobbin and top threads by sewing several hand-tacking stitches.

On the second pillowcase I used three pastel machine embroidery thread colors. I programmed "NOW I LAY ME DOWN TO SLEEP" into the memory and stitched it over and over across the hem on the three lines I drew. I like the quilted look at the hems, though you might want to forego the batting and opt for a flat hem. You can also stitch your sentiments on doubled ruffle before folding, gathering, and attaching it to the edge of the pillow.

Stitch sheet hems, too, to match.

VARIATIONS:

Stitch in a personal name, including all the nicknames you know the person answers to. Or write down all the remembrances you have of a particular person—vacation spots, birthdate, favorite food, movie, ice cream, sports, teacher, dog's name—you get the idea. What about a white-on-white pillowcase, with names and wedding date and more memories? These pillowcases take only minutes to make, and what conversation pieces they can be!

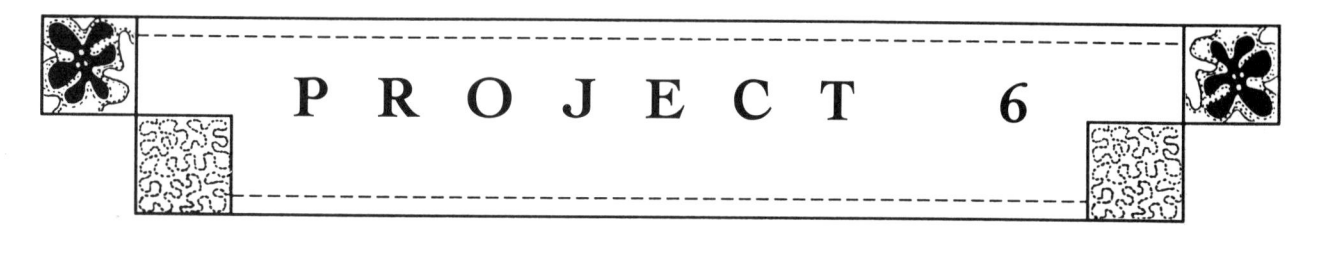
Petticoat Lampshade Cover

This is an ancient idea for covering a small lampshade. My mother didn't invent them, but she made them so often through the years that her name should go on them instead of the real one: petticoat cover. She showed me how and now I make them, too, because they are easy, super-fast, and a pattern isn't needed. I've revamped the construction, now that I'm a serger person, but using a sewing machine is fine. When I mention a serger in the directions, you can use your sewing machine to seam and use zigzag or serpentine (multiple zigzag) stitches to finish the edges.

First measure the plain shade on your lamp. You'll need to know the circumference of it at the top, the bottom, and the height of the shade measured along the slant of the shade (Fig. 1.54). (I like these covers best on shades that are narrower at the top than at the bottom.)

Let's use my small shade as an example (Fig. 1.55): At the top the circumference is 21″ (53.5cm), at the bottom it's 34″ (86.5cm). The shade is 9″ (23cm) along the slant. With these measurements you can cut the fabrics for the shade cover and lining, both the same size.

There is a 1″ (2.5cm) ruffle at the top, under that a ½″ (1.3cm) casing for ribbon,

YOU WILL NEED:

Fabric: Top and lining (see above)

Needle: #80/12 universal

Thread: Matching sewing

Presser feet: Zig-zag (0); buttonhole (3)

Miscellaneous: Vanishing marker; Yardstick; ⅜″ (9.5mm) grosgrain ribbon to match (length = circumference of upper lampshade + 36″ [.95m]); 1″ × ½″ (2.5cm × 1.3cm) iron-on interfacing; Aleene's Stop Fraying

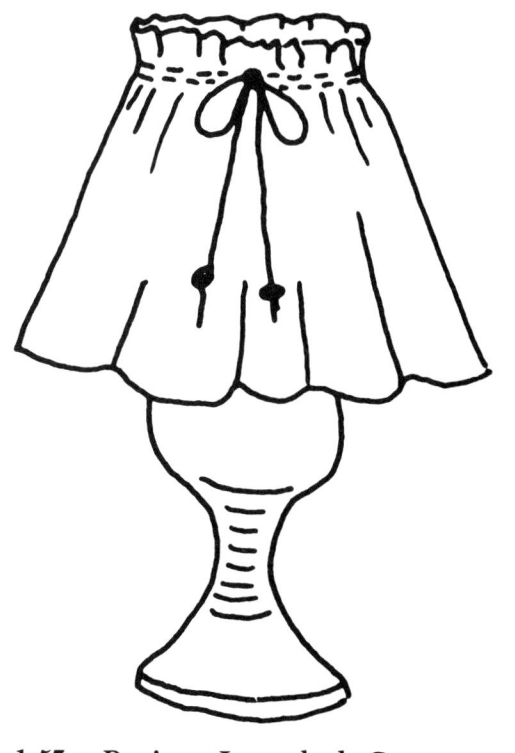

1.53 ▪ Petticoat Lampshade Cover.

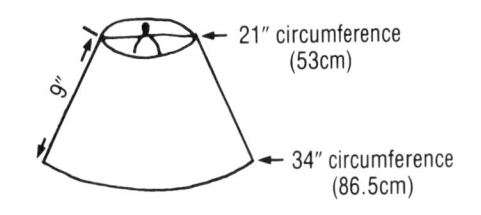

1.54 ▪ Take measurements of the circumference at top and bottom, and the height of the lampshade to make your own lampshade cover.

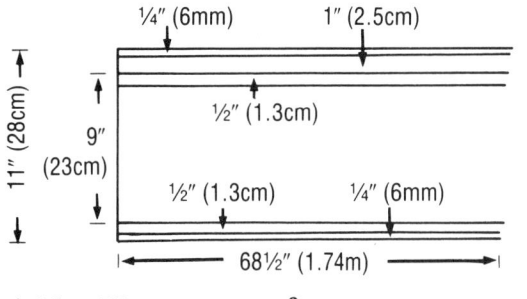

1.55 ▪ Measurements for my lampshade cover.

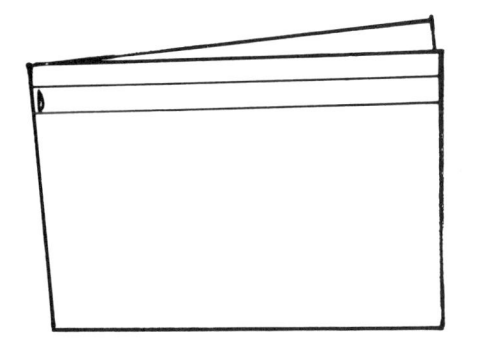

1.56 ▪ Fold lampshade cover in half to find buttonhole placement.

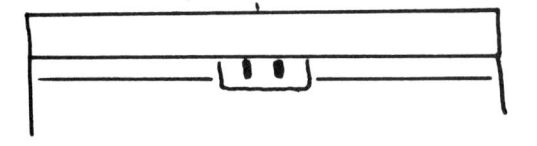

1.57 ▪ Back buttonhole placement with fusible interfacing.

9″ (23cm) for the shade, and ½″ (1.3cm) overhang. Therefore, the length of the fabric is 1″ + 9″ (2.5cm + 23cm) + ½″ (1.3cm) overhang; add ½″ (1.3cm) for two ¼″ (6mm) seam allowances, for a total of 11″ (28cm). Width is predicated on the circumference at the lower edge, 34″ (86.5cm), which is doubled; 68″ (1.65m) + ½″ (1.3cm) for seam allowances = 68½″ (1.75m).

Cut out both pieces of fabric, for shade cover and lining, 11″ × 68½″ (28cm × 1.75m). If you must piece fabric, it won't be noticeable because seams are lost in the gathers and don't show.

Prepare the front of the lampshade by drawing stitching lines 1¼″ (3cm) from the top edge of your fabric and ½″ (1.3cm) down from the first line to create the ribbon casing. To find the center and place the buttonholes, place the cut edges of the shade cover together and fold the fabric in half the short way (Fig. 1.56). Mark two lines for vertical buttonholes in the ribbon casing area, one on either side of the fold, leaving about ¼″ (6mm) between buttonholes. Iron on a scrap of fusible interfacing behind the buttonhole marks (Fig. 1.57), then use your sewing machine with thread to match the lampshade fabric to make buttonholes. Open the buttonholes.

Next, place the top sides of the front and lining fabrics together and serge both long edges, using ¼″ (6mm) seams (Fig. 1.58). Turn the tube to the right side and press top and bottom seams.

Take the lampshade back to your sewing machine and straight-stitch both marked casing lines (Fig. 1.59).

The length of the ⅜″ (9.5cm) grosgrain ribbon is estimated by using the top lampshade measurement (21″ [53.5cm]) and adding 36″ (.95m) for the bow. First, cut the ribbon in half. Thread one piece through the casing from the cut edge of the lampshade cover through the buttonhole. Repeat on the other side. Pull out just a bit beyond the edge and pin (Fig. 1.60). Place right sides of the tube together, pin, and serge the edges together.

Turn the lampshade cover to the right side. Pull up on the ribbon and gather the top to fit your lampshade. Tie the ribbon into a bow. Trim the ribbon ends to the length you wish and use Stop Fraying at the edges. Now, what could be more simple? I think I'll make another one!

VARIATIONS:

1. Use organdy and hem-stitches. (Scallop the edges for a great look, or use an edge-scalloped embroidered fabric.)

2. Run a ribbon or elastic casing at the top and bottom (this works especially well with a lampshade that is the same width at the top and bottom).

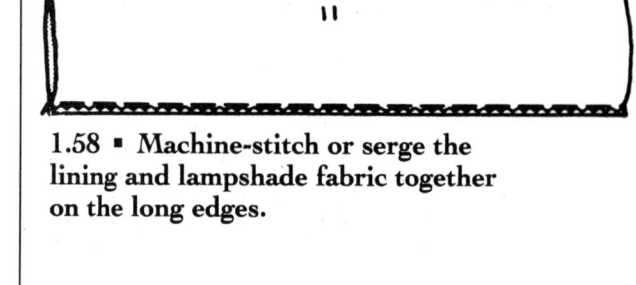

1.58 ▪ Machine-stitch or serge the lining and lampshade fabric together on the long edges.

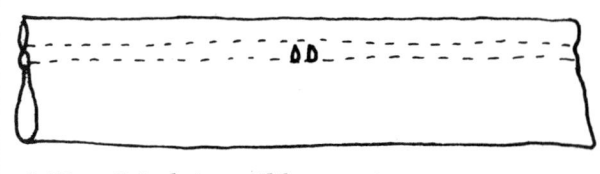

1.59 ▪ Stitch in a ribbon casing.

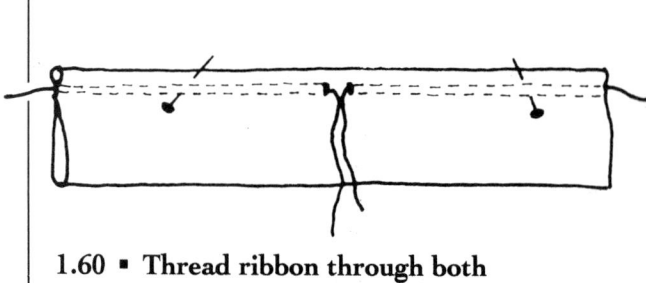

1.60 ▪ Thread ribbon through both sides before serging the lampshade cover into a circle.

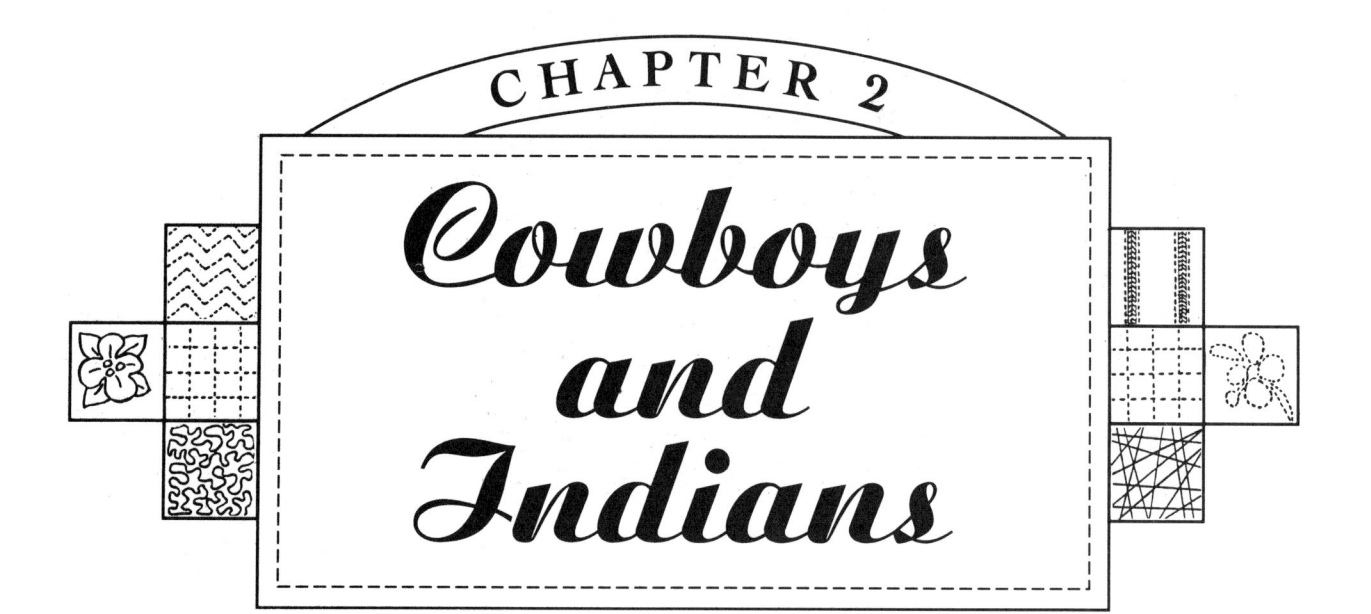

CHAPTER 2
Cowboys and Indians

Southwest colors have always appealed to me—even before this decorating style took the country by storm. Rusts, turquoise, teal, brown, and sand are the basics I used in this chapter. For two pillows and a headboard, I used leather and suede for fabric, as well as synthetic leather (Ultrasuede). Don't shy away from stitching these. Follow my directions and you'll find them not only extremely easy, but enjoyable to stitch—no folding under edges, and leather needles cut through the toughest cowhide like butter. Included also are fabric pillows, and I've added a wreath and Indian doll for the fun of it.

45

Leather Patched Headboard

Make this in one of two ways. Cover a headboard that's on your bed, or make a quilted headboard like this one to hang on the wall behind your bed. This one fits a twin bed. Instead of making it exactly 39″ (9.9m)—twin bed size—I added 2″ (5.1cm) to keep it from looking skimpy.

Stitch a background of leather and suede together to equal the measurement you need. Use polyester thread for the bobbin, clear monofilament on top, and stitch length 4. To attach the leathers, first overlap them ¼″ (6mm) and stitch close to the edge. (I stitched by lining up the inside of the presser foot with the edge of the leather first, then placing the presser foot on the edge and stitching again.)

Cut out appliqués from Ultrasuede and

YOU WILL NEED:

Fabric: leather, suede, Ultrasuede (buy old coats and skirts at thrift stores, or order from Tandy (see "Sources of Supplies," page 93) to cover 41″ × 24″ (10.4m x 61cm), heavy brown backing fabric (45″ x 28″ [11.3m × 7.1m])

Needle: #110/18 leather needle

Thread: polyester sewing, clear mono-filament

Presser feet: Teflon (52), roller (51), or walking foot (50); bulky over-lock (12)

Miscellaneous: Pellon fleece 41″ × 24″ (10.4m x 61cm); rotary cutter and mat; and 6″ x 24″ (15cm × 61cm) clear plastic ruler, 4 yards (3.5m) purchased brown, leather-like covered cable cord or make your own; glue stick, thick tacky glue, 45″ × ½″ (11.4m × 13cm) dowel, clip clothespins or kitchen clips

2.1 ▪ Draw a guide for appliqué placement when you make a headboard.

2.2 to 2.8 • Use these appliqué ideas and those in Figs. 2.12–2.14.

leathers and arrange them on the top. Dot glue stick behind them. Then stitch at the edge of the appliqués to attach—you don't have to turn under the edges. Use the Teflon, roller, or walking foot. Try each and decide which one you like the best.

Then add fleece to the back of the headboard and quilt in place from the front by using stitch-in-the-ditch at the edge of each shape.

Assemble the headboard by first placing the edge of the presser foot at the top edge of the piece you just completed. Stitch all around the perimeter of the fleece. Trim the leather to match the size of the fleece.

Use the bulky overlock foot to attach the covered cable cord around the front edge of the headboard.

Cut out seven 2″ × 5½″ (5cm × 14cm) leather strips for hanging loops. Fold the strips in half the short way, and dot with glue to hold them together. Space them evenly across the top edge of the headboard and stitch.

Cut out the backing fabric and place it, right sides together, on top of the headboard. (I always add extra fabric backing to thick, quilted projects to prevent future fitting surprises.) Stitch the edges from the front, using the bulky overlock foot. Use needle position to place the stitching just inside the stitching line that's already there. Because you're using leather, it is extremely difficult to pin the backing in place, so try this method: Center the backing fabric at the top of the headboard and stitch across. Stop,

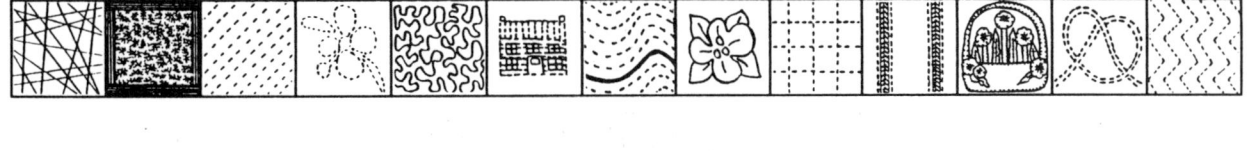

2.9 ▪ Stitch seven leather loops at the top of the headboard.

2.10 ▪ Attach the lining by sewing within stitching lines already there.

take the wallhanging off the machine, and place it on a flat surface. Smooth it out and cut away the extra backing fabric from the next side you sew. Smooth, trim, and stitch each side. Leave at least 6″ (15cm) open at the bottom of the headboard for turning right side out.

Once all four sides are completed, turn it right side out. Glue the opening closed with thick tacky glue. Hold the layers together with large clips or clip clothespins until dry.

Quilt the appliqués and backing together by stitching just outside the edges of the appliqués to attach the layers together.

Slip a large dowel through the loops and hang at the head of the bed.

YOU WILL NEED:

Fabric: Leather, suede, and Ultra-suede scraps to cover 14″ (35.6cm) square plus appliqués; 16″ × 14″ (40.6cm × 35.6cm) leather piece or combine scraps for backing

Needle: #110/18 leather

Thread: polyester sewing thread, clear monofilament

Presser foot: Teflon (52), roller (51), and/or walking foot (50); bulky overlock (12)

Miscellaneous: 14″ (35.6cm) pillow form; glue stick; rotary cutter and mat; 6″ × 24″ (15cm × 61cm) clear plastic ruler; 4″ (10cm)-wide purchased suede or leather fringe or make your own; 12″ (30.5cm) Velcro strips; fiberfill (optional); Pellon fleece (optional)

Leather Appliqué Pillows

After you make the headboard, make these pillows to match.

Using monofilament, construct the pillows as you did the headboard (Project 7), first stitching scraps together (14″ [35.6cm] square) for the top and backing, and then stitching appliqués to the pillow top.

Place fleece behind the appliquéd pillow top if you wish. Stitch at the edge of the appliqués and background shapes to quilt and attach the layers.

To make the backing, cut the backing fabric in half (2 pieces 8″ × 14″ [20.5cm ×

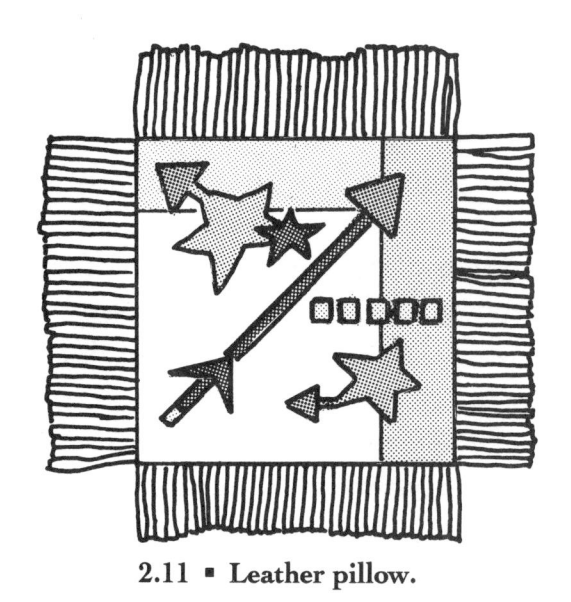

2.11 ▪ Leather pillow.

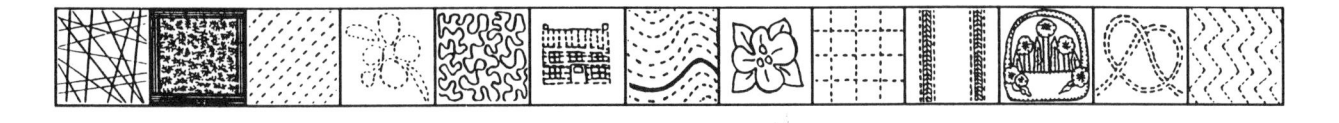

35.6cm]). Fold under the long side of one piece of leather or suede, if it is soft enough. If you are using soft suede, back it first with scrap fabric to strengthen it. Fold under the other side, or add a piece of leather or cowhide on top of the cut edge and sew in place to reinforce the edge.

Using polyester thread, stitch the Velcro strips to the top of one edge and the underside of the other. Then press the Velcro together and stitch the two sides together at each end as shown. Put aside.

Next, cut out fringe strips. Do this by cutting strips of leather 4″ (10cm) wide. Fringe is easily assembled from scraps butted together. With a rotary cutter, mat, and ruler, cut ¼″ (6mm)-wide fringe up to almost the top. I left approximately ¼″ (6mm) uncut at the top.

With a disappearing pen and ruler, underneath the pillow front, mark a line ½″ (13cm) from the edge all around. Brush glue stick on that edge and place the right side of the edge of the fringe on the line you've drawn—fringe extending beyond the pillow.

Place pillow sides wrong sides together and use the glue stick again to hold the two pillow pieces together. With monofilament, stitch on the top edge around the pillow, ⅛″ (3mm) from the edge. Then go back and stitch again ¼″ (6cm) from the first line of stitching.

Open the Velcro and slip the pillow form inside. If the corners need more filling, use handfuls of loose fiberfill.

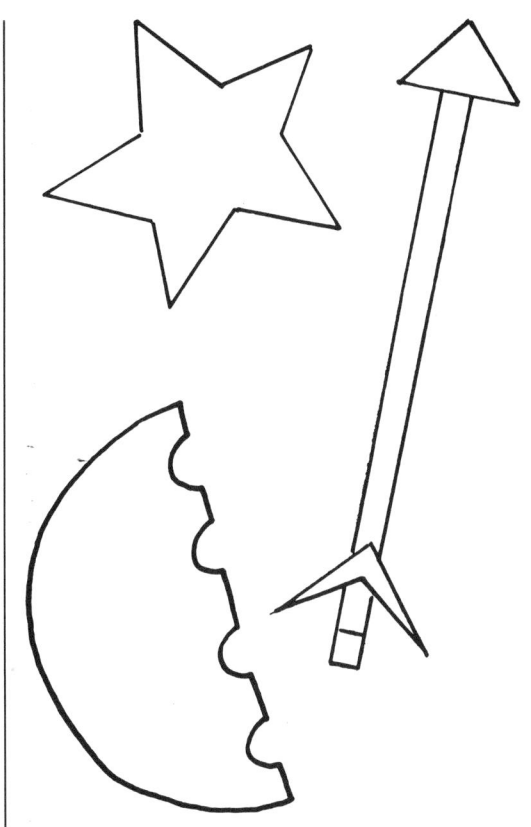

2.12 to 2.14 ▪ Use these appliqué ideas and those in Figs. 2.2–2.28.

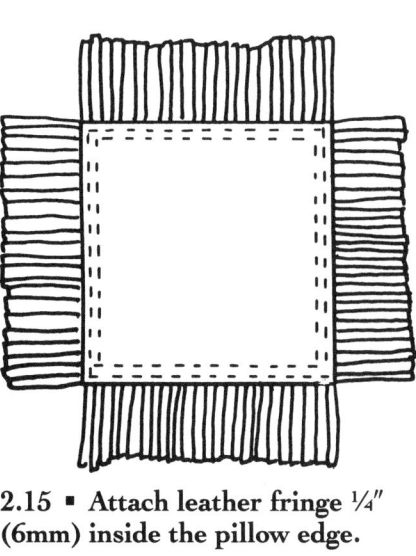

2.15 ▪ Attach leather fringe ¼″ (6mm) inside the pillow edge.

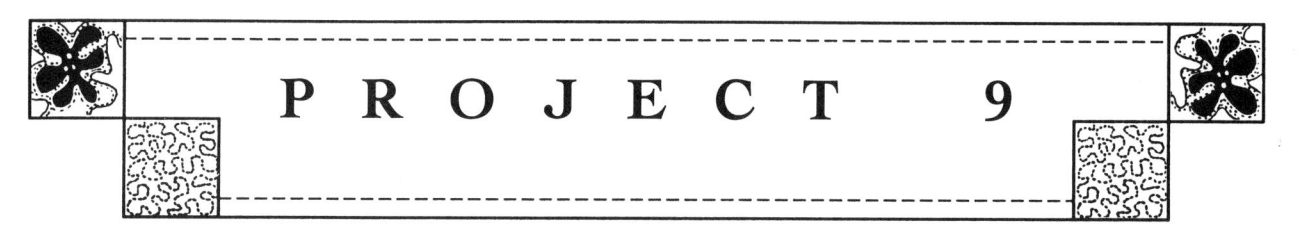

P R O J E C T   9

YOU WILL NEED:

Fabric: two pieces of print fabric the size of the pillow form

Needle: #80/12 universal, hand-sewing

Thread: sewing to match or coordinate with the fabric; clear monofilament (optional)

Presser foot: zigzag (0), walking foot (50)

Miscellaneous: Pellon fusible fleece—size to match pillow front and back; pillow form; beads, suede strips, leather laces, conchos, arrowheads, decorative pins for decoration, twine (4′ [1.2m]); tacky glue; pinback

2.16 ▪ Quilt-the-Print Pillow.

Quilting-the-Print Pillow

This is the quickest, easiest way to make a quilted pillow. All you have to do is back a piece of printed fabric with batting and straight stitch the printed design with either presser foot on, feed dogs up, or free-quilting foot on with feed dogs lowered.

First back both sides of the pillow with fusible fleece and press to fuse. With the walking foot on, stitch in the design of the fabric using either sewing thread or clear monofilament. This is an easy fabric to quilt because it has long, straight lines. Complete both sides.

With right sides together, stitch or serge around the edge of the pillow, leaving enough opening at the bottom edge to turn the pillow and insert a pillow form.

Cut the twine into four pieces. Before turning the pillow top, grab a handful of corner fabric (about 4″ [10cm]) and tie it off tightly with a piece of the twine. Repeat at each corner. Then turn the case to the right side, insert the pillow form, and stitch up the opening by hand. Without a back opening, the pillow is usable from either side, and there's no need to fill out corners with added fiberfill.

But we can't leave well-enough alone, can we? It still needs something. Buttons? Rib-

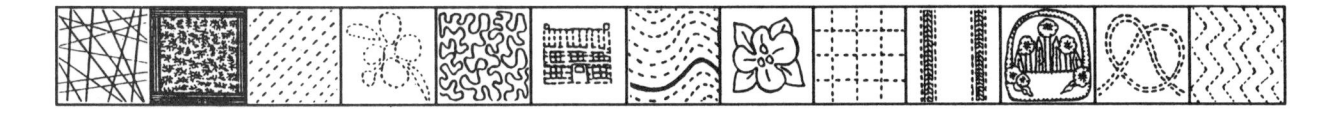

bon? Lace? More stitches? It depends on the pillow's purpose, the print, and whether that something extra would add or detract. I thought it added to this pillow, so I added a long fringed decoration that I can attach to the pillow with the pin I glued on to its back or remove when I want to wash the pillow top.

If you want to make a decoration, too, then visit a craft department and find dozens of cowboy and Indian ideas. A concho? Leather belt circles? Fringe? Beads? Arrowheads? Buy what you think you can use, adding bits and pieces from what you already own. Cut strips of suede from scraps, gather small twigs from the yard, or if you have a birch tree that sheds, as we do, then gather up the bark (cut into stars or moons, birds, even coyotes). Start playing around with all the components you have. Try one thing and another until you're pleased with the pin you create.

I started with a heavy leather circle, and placed a large turquoise disk (an Egyptian paste doo-dad a friend gave me) on it. Over this I placed a concho. All these layers are tied together with two leather laces threaded from the back through the circle, disk, concho, and back again through the layers.

I added three narrow 24″ (61cm)-long strips of suede by finding the middle of them and gluing that with tacky glue to the back of the leather circle. I put this collection of suede and concho aside to dry.

While the glue was drying, I prepared the rest of the decoration. I cut out two pieces of

2.17 ▪ **Tie pillow corners with twine.**

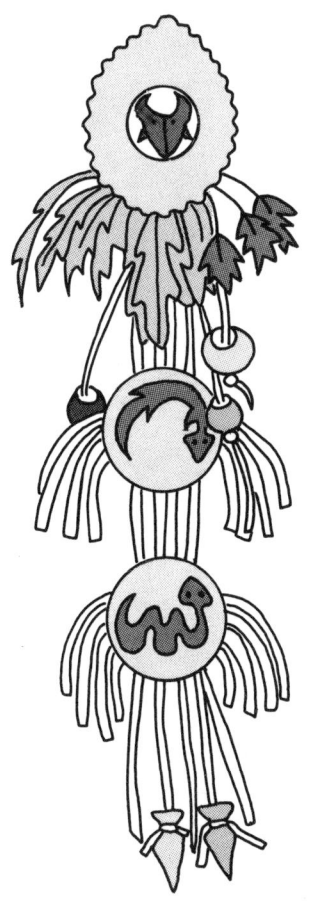

2.18 ▪ **Decorative pin for the pillow.**

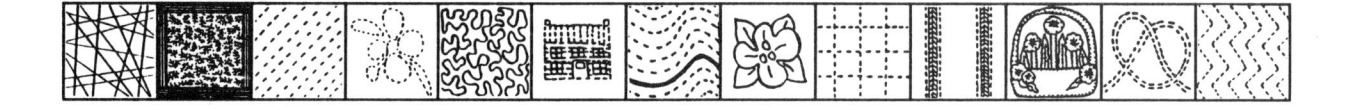

2.19 ▪ **Reinforce glued pin back by gluing a piece of fabric over the pin and on to the decoration.**

chamois, each $1'' \times 6''$ (2.5cm x 15cm). Using the rotary cutter and mat, I fringed each side of the rectangles. Then I glued these to the back of two disks of Egyptian paste. On the front of all three turquoise disks I glued purchased silver metal decorations (first flattening the points at the edges of the decorations).

To finish the pin, I glued the two disks to the long leather and suede strips attached to the top leather circle. The middle disk is $4''$ (10cm) from the top one to allow space for the feathers I added. Those I dipped into glue and pushed up under the top disk. The bottom disk is glued $3''$ (7.5cm) from the middle one.

Glue the jewelry pin to the underside of the leather top with thick tacky glue. Then spread glue on a tiny piece of scrap fabric or suede ($3/4'' \times 1\frac{1}{2}''$ [2cm $\times$ 4cm]) and press it down over the flat front of the jewelry pin so the pin won't pop off.

Add beads and arrowheads by stringing the beads through the leather laces and tying overhand knots to hold the beads on, and by tying the arrowheads on the suede strips with overhand knots. Place a dot of glue under the knots.

Once all the glue is dry, pin the decoration to your pillow to take it out of the ordinary.

Clipped and Quilted Pillow

Texture created by cutting through many quilted layers dates back hundreds of years, but it's been rediscovered and made more exciting by new and different fabrics. I decided to use this method for a pillow. Six fabrics lie under the top layer. After quilting, the top and fabric underneath are slashed. Edges fray, colors peek out, and your home gains a unique texture.

Traditionally, you draw in squares, rectangles, and zigzag lines to slash on the top fabric. I chose instead a printed fabric with squares and rectangles as part of the design.

To add more interest and more designs to slash, the top was constructed from two triangles. Each triangle was chosen for having interesting designs for clipping. The first one was cut from the 18″ (46cm) square. A

YOU WILL NEED:

Fabric: one piece of printed fabric 33″ × 27″ (84cm x 68.6cm) cut in two pieces: 18″ (46cm) square and 27″ × 15″ (68.6cm × 38cm); one piece for backing (20″ [51cm] square); 6 plain fabrics in coordinating colors to top print (18″ [46cm] square), 6 plain fabrics same colors as first 6 (27″ × 15″ [68.6cm × 38cm])—all in coordinating colors. (You need a total of 12 different plain fabrics, each 33″ × 27″ (84cm × 68.6cm)

Thread: sewing thread to coordinate with the print

Needle: #90/14 sharp (jeans)

Presser foot: zigzag (0), walking foot (50), bulky overlock (12), zipper (4)

Miscellaneous: sharp embroidery scissors; 18″ (46cm) square pillow form, ready-made covered cord for edge (or make your own), dressmaker's pins

2.20 ▪ Clipped and quilted pillow.

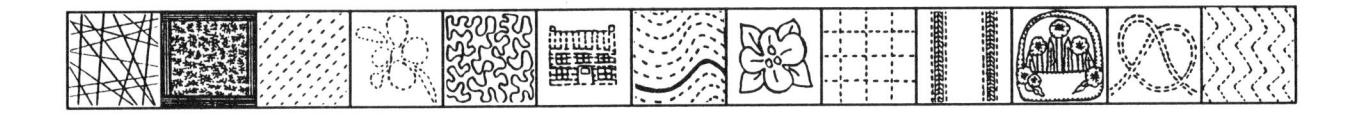

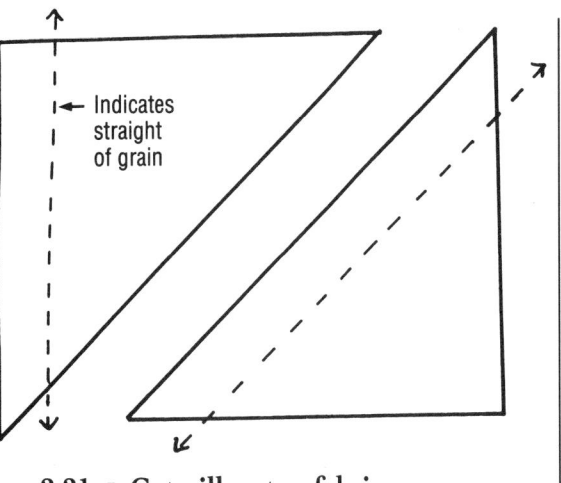

2.21 ▪ **Cut pillow top fabric.**

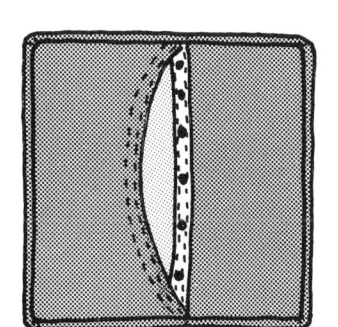

2.22 ▪ **Use snap tape for the pillow opening.**

line was cut diagonally from the lower left-hand corner to the upper righthand corner (the straight of grain follows the side of the square). Use only the triangle at left; put the other one aside.

The other triangle used for the pillow was cut as shown in Fig. 2.21. The straight of grain follows the pillow's center seam. Stitch the triangles together.

The other pieces of fabric are cut and layered underneath the top print, following the same grain lines as the top fabrics. Pin all the layers together, but don't seam them—it eliminates bulk. From the top, stitch in the long design lines to hold the layers together. Remove the pins and stitch in the shorter lines. When the stitching is complete, sew around the edges of the pillow top to hold the layers together.

Slashing must be done on the fabric bias instead of the straight so the raw edges are fluffy, not ravelled.

Choose which areas to cut. Use a sharp, short embroidery scissors to cut to, but not through, the bottom layer. If you slip and cut through the bottom layer, iron on scraps of mending tape or fusible interfacing underneath.

Once cut, soak the top in water, then put it into the dryer to fluff. The more you wet and dry it, the more the edges will fluff.

Finish the pillow like the Victorian pillows in Project 3, where snap tape is used for the closure. But instead of ruffles, stitch covered cord around the edges before you assemble the pillow pieces.

Western Wreath

Purchase an 18″ (46cm) wreath to decorate. I always look at them as if they were blank canvases. What will the theme be? How can I make this one different? What colors shall I use?

Wrap the wreath with the 6″ (15cm)-wide fabric, leaving some wreath exposed. As you wrap, crunch the fabric a bit, slipping the raw edges under. Use the glue gun to glue the end of the fabric inside the wreath from the back. Glue again at any join and at the end. Do all the joining behind the wreath unless you place a decoration over a join on front. Glue anywhere you must to keep the fabric in place.

Then let your imagination go. Take out all those feathers, beads, suede strips, and

YOU WILL NEED:
Wreath: purchased 18″ (46cm) grapevine
Decorations: your choice 6″ × 2¾ yards (15cm × 2.5m)-wide fabric to wrap the wreath, suede and wool fabric scraps, suede laces, conchos, leather belt pieces, stars, feathers, beads, twigs, birch bark
Miscellaneous: thick tacky glue, glue gun, wire for hanging

2.23 ▪ Western wreath.

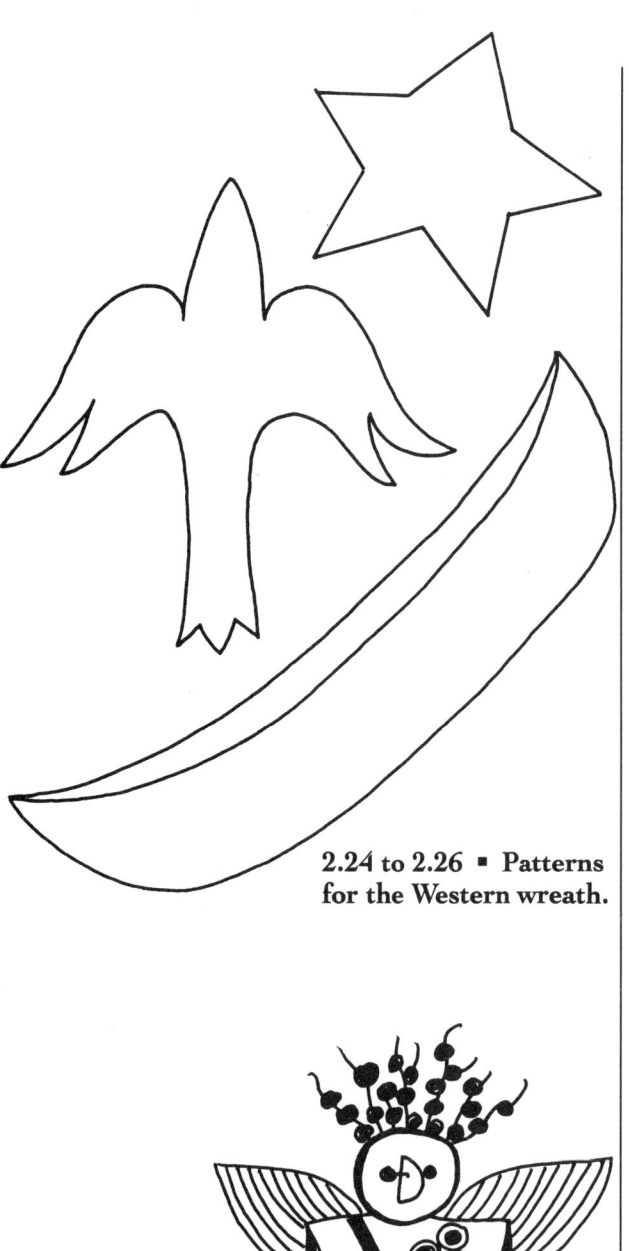

2.24 to 2.26 ▪ Patterns for the Western wreath.

2.27 ▪ Bird fetish decoration.

leather laces again and start combining them into decorations for the wreath.

Find twigs, wrap and tie them in suede, and glue them to the wreath. Add a decoration to the suede knot.

To make other decorations for the wreath, use your choice of the following decorating ideas: Cut out your choice of stars, moon, canoes, coyotes, and birds from suede or wool (cut two sides), stitch them together, leaving a few inches open to fill them with fiberfill. Finish the seam. Then go back by hand and overcast the edges with fine leather lacing or thick thread to make it look as backwoods as the rest of the wreath.

Or cut patterns from cardboard and cover with fabric or suede. Use birch bark if you're lucky enough to have access to it (strengthen the bark by spreading glue on the back; then glue it to a piece of fabric and trim around the edge of the design). Glue these designs to the wreath with a glue gun or thick tacky glue.

Add a bird fetish made from a triangle of wool fabric. Arms and feet are made of twigs, the wings are clam shells, and he's decorated with beads. His face is a wooden button and the beak is a turquoise stone. (For more information on this kind of decoration, see *How to Make Soft Jewelry* and *Gifts Galore,* by Jane Warnick and myself.)

Twist wire or tie cord at the back for a hanger and use it in your cowboys and Indians room.

Indian Chief Doll

You'll never make only one of these dolls: They are quick and easy to construct, decorating them is so much fun, and the results are wonderful. There isn't much sewing, but this Indian will add fun to your cowboys and Indians decor. Don't be limited by the size of this pattern. Once you read through the directions and understand how the doll is constructed, you can readily comprehend how to make any size. One of the simplest ways to reduce or enlarge the size is to use a copy machine with those features.

I've made these dolls using suede, scraps

YOU WILL NEED:

Fabric: for the body, your choice of leather, wool, or cotton (13″ × 8″ [33cm × 20cm]; for the base, 6″ (15cm) square suede, chamois or felt; 6″ (15cm) square suede for head covering

Needle: appropriate for fabric choice, hand-sewing

Thread: clear monofilament, sewing (appropriate for fabric)

Presser foot: zigzag (0)

Miscellaneous: heavy mat board (6″ [15cm]); fur scraps; your choice of bells, porcupine quills, fetishes, stones, tiny pinecones, beads, feathers, shells, suede strips and scraps, leather laces, yarns and cords for decorations; roving yarn (or yarn of your choice) for hair; fiberfill; small round or egg-shaped Styrofoam ball; or Sculpey clay for head (optional); thick tacky glue; red blush makeup and permanent markers

2.28 ▪ Indian doll.

COWBOYS AND INDIANS 58

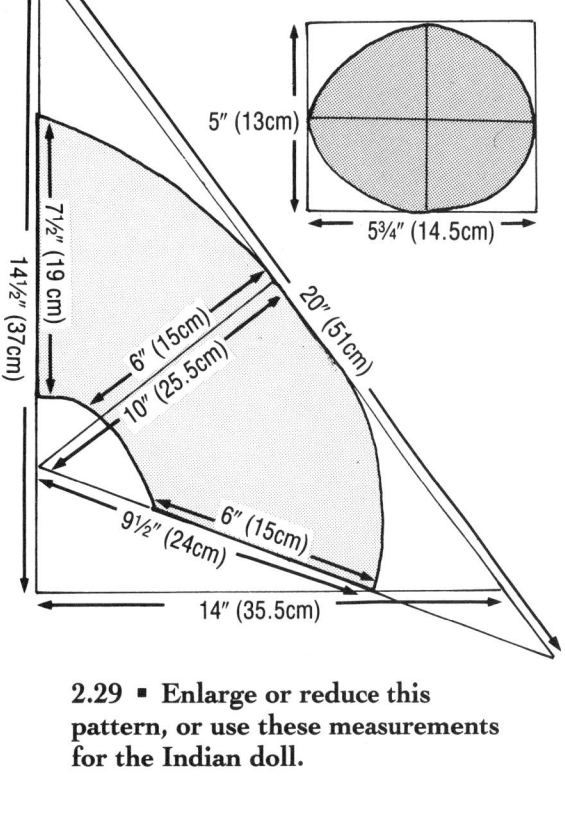

2.29 ▪ Enlarge or reduce this pattern, or use these measurements for the Indian doll.

2.30 ▪ Stay stitch across the top and bottom edges.

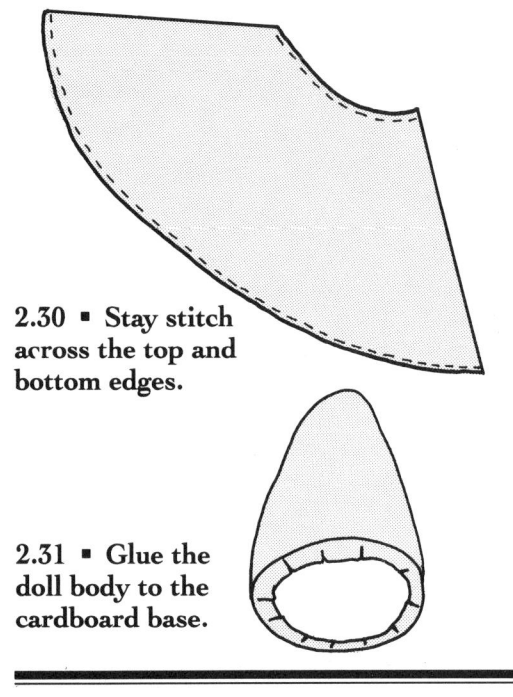

2.31 ▪ Glue the doll body to the cardboard base.

of a wool Indian rug, and cotton, and discovered that stiff fabrics aren't as successful as soft.

Trace this pattern from the book (Fig. 2.29), enlarging or reducing it on a copy machine; or start with the triangle and rectangle as shown in the same figure, using the measurements as given. Place the body pattern on your fabric and cut it out. Copy the base on mat board, then copy again on leather, suede, or felt.

To make the body, use your Bernina to stay stitch ¼″ (6.4mm) around the top and bottom curves of the body. Overlap the edges of the body ½″ (13cm), pin, then stitch it together by hand. If you've chosen a cotton or wool fabric, either fold under a seam allowance or plan to glue a leather strip or decorative braid on top of the cut edge. Sometimes I add more fabric to the front edge so I can fringe the extension after sewing the seam. You can slip a strip of fringe inside the edge before you sew it in place. The easiest decoration? Whipstitch the raw edges closed with a contrasting, yet coordinating sewing thread. Make the stitches long (½″ [13cm]) and let them add to the decor.

To make a base, spread glue ¼″ (6.4mm) in around the edge of the cardboard base. Glue side out, slip this inside the fabric you've sewn, placing the pointed end of the cardboard base at or slightly ahead of the fabric seam. Finger press the edges of the fabric to the glued bottom edge of the cardboard (your line of stay-stitching helps). Add more glue if needed. Press the fabric as flat

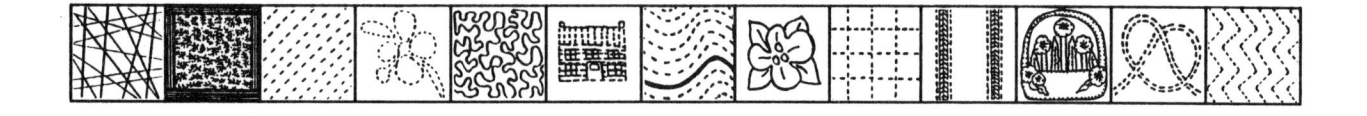

as possible, clipping and removing any pleats that may keep your doll from standing flat. Next, sew on the suede or felt piece by hand, using a contrasting, yet coordinating color thread—I use the same thread to sew the edges of the body fabric in place. Instead of trying to hide the stitches, again make them part of the decoration by stitching them long and obvious (at least ¼" [6.4mm]). Now fill the body with fiberfill. It's possible to shape the body somewhat at this time if you wish. Put this part of the doll aside.

Make the head next. You have several options. First, you can cover a Styrofoam ball with suede and tie the suede together underneath the head, then attach it to the body by pushing the extra suede down into the top hole of the doll's body. If the styrofoam egg is too large, roll it on the table, applying hand pressure as you do. This crushes the Styrofoam and you can roll it to the size and shape you want. I especially like this type of head because I can add a bit of glue to the face area of the Styrofoam, and when the suede is stretched over it, I can pinch the suede together for a nose, creating more shape to the face. It's also possible to push in eye sockets, then stitch black beads inside them. Finish the face by coloring with red blush makeup and marking pens.

Fiberfill is another head option, and perhaps the fastest. Cover a tight wad of fiberfill with suede, tie off at the bottom, and poke into the neck hole of the doll. Draw on a face with permanent markers, add blush, and use beads for eyes.

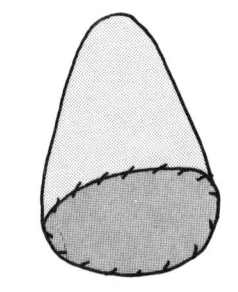

2.32 ▪ **Attach fabric base by hand, sewing it to the doll body.**

2.33 ▪ **Cover head shape with suede and tie under the chin.**

2.34 ▪ Wrap braids with strip of narrow suede.

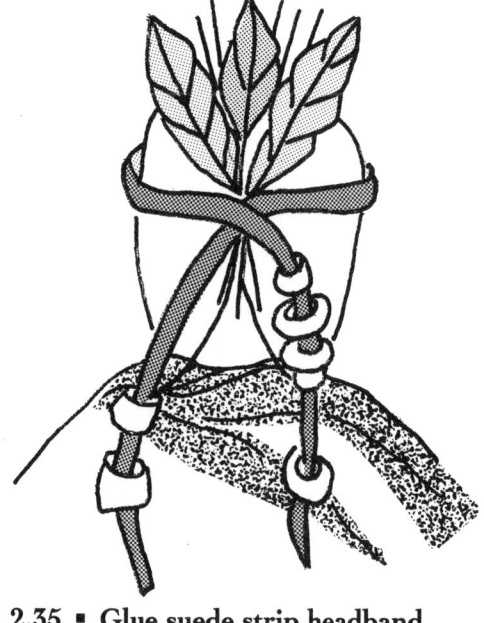

2.35 ▪ Glue suede strip headband together; then add beads and feathers.

Sculpey is easily worked, and doesn't have to be perfect, as it'll be covered with suede. Make an egg-shaped head (you can mold a nose and chin if you wish). After baking to harden it, cover the head with suede and pull the suede tightly down underneath and tie it off as you did the others. Decorate the face as you did the previous ones. Let your imagination soar.

Once the head is completed and the suede ends are down inside the neck opening, keep the head in place by wrapping around the neck with sewing thread and tying securely (you can decorate this later if you wish). Glue braids of roving or yarn of your choice (narrow suede strips work well, as do tiny torn strips of black fabric) to the head for hair.

Wrap the braids with narrow strips of suede, dip feathers into glue, and slip them into the overhand knots at the ends of the braids.

Use a suede strip as a headband. Glue it around the head and let the ends dangle from the back. (Add beads there if you wish or cut these ends off later.) Glue three small feathers (even porcupine quills) inside the band at the back.

Now the decorating fun begins. Glue a scrap of fur around the doll's shoulders, and add strings of beads, feathers, fetishes, bells, and shells to cords, suede strips, or leather laces. Let them dangle from around the neck or from under the fur robe.

Make Indians in several sizes for a table grouping—what attention-grabbers!

61 INDIAN CHIEF DOLL

CHAPTER 3

The 90s Are Now!

"Now" colors are zingy, electric confetti colors that zap the eye and make you smile. Okay, sometimes they make you laugh. They're the colors that look like clowns love them—they look like fun.

I want to sleep under the duvet/summer quilt. In fact, walking into the room with that on the bed, with the patched sham on the pillow, makes me feel good.

Something's needed on the wall, so you'll find a small picture using my favorite, easy way to appliqué with print fabrics and bridal tulle.

Big black ants running over the red and white tablecloth inspired me to quilt a picnic cloth, which is more mat than tablecloth. It's easily constructed using the log cabin quilt pattern with a courthouse steps assembly. Starting at the center laminated-fabric square, the red denim strips with pockets for silverware are added to the sides. Then a quilted seating area is stitched around the four sides. What fun! Let's go out to the backyard and test this thing.

PROJECT   **1 3**

YOU WILL NEED:

Three twin flat sheets

Fabric: ½ yard (46cm) of seven fabrics for colored areas, ¼ yard (22.9cm) of seven contrasting fabrics for edge strips on the quilt

Thread: polyester sewing thread the color of the top sheet, clear monofilament

Presser foot: zigzag (0), walking foot (50), open embroidery (20), patchwork (37), Fasturn foot accessory (optional)

Miscellaneous: rotary cutter, mat, 6″ × 24″ (15cm x 61cm) clear plastic ruler, low-loft bonded batting for twin bed, quilting pins, safety pins, yardstick, disappearing marker, 69″ (1.75m) Velcro, Fasturn tools (optional)

Duvet Cover/ Summer Quilt Combo

Our family was discussing what kind of bedding to take to the lake in northern Wisconsin for an early summer vacation. We've been there when it was so cold I bought extra blankets, yet there have been warmer nights, too, when all we needed was a light cover. "What we need," I said, "is a heavy quilt that, on command, transforms itself into

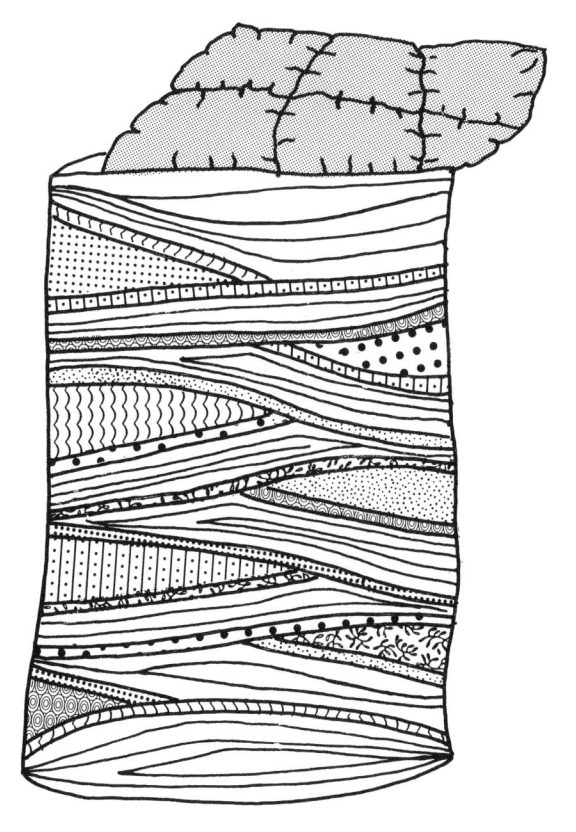

3.1 ▪ Duvet Cover.

63   DUVET COVER/SUMMER QUILT COMBO

a light cover." No, I didn't shout "Eureka!" but I thought of a duvet and duvet cover.

The duvet, or quilt, sounded perfect for freezing cold nights, but if there's only a slight chill, we need something heavier than the usual sheet-weight duvet cover. So the idea evolved into adding batting to the top sheet cover and quilting it. We can use the light summer quilt on cool nights and we can open the Velcro at the top and slip the duvet inside when the temperature plummets.

I bought a duvet and then I made a duvet cover/summer quilt combo I can slip it into.

To make the cover, I purchased two red twin flat sheets (get them at a discount store) instead of buying fabric I'd have to piece together. Sheeting is available by the yard at some fabric stores, so this is a consideration.

Actually, I needed three sheets for this combo, but one won't show, so for the third sheet, I used an old one I already had. If you don't have an old sheet, buy one at a thrift shop.

The duvet measures 68″ × 88″ (1.72m × 2.2m); the standard twin sheet is 66″ × 96″ (1.67m × 2.4m). I felt the smaller width of the sheet was acceptable, as the duvet plumped up inside. Instead of cutting off the sheet lengths to match the duvet, I left the extra fabric in place because the top is folded over 2″ (5cm) and the closure at the top also uses length, as does the seam allowance. The thickness of the duvet fills the cover beautifully.

The machine-quilting technique combines

3.2 ▪ Sew appliqués on top of sheet and batting.

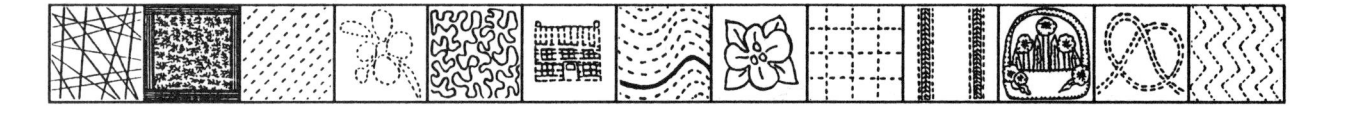

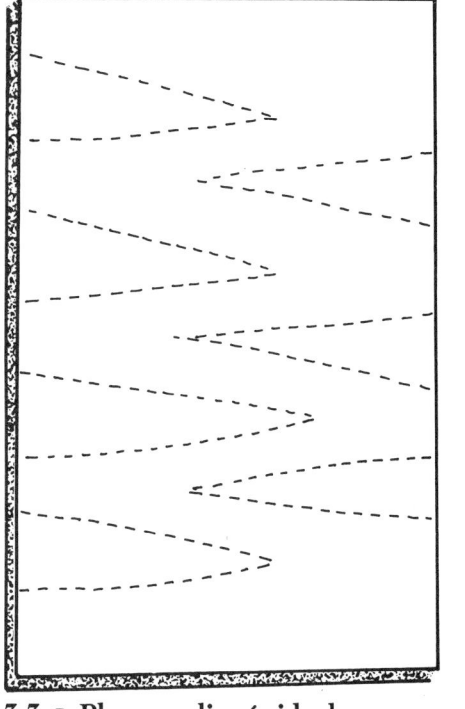

3.3 ▪ Place appliqué side down on underside of top sheet.

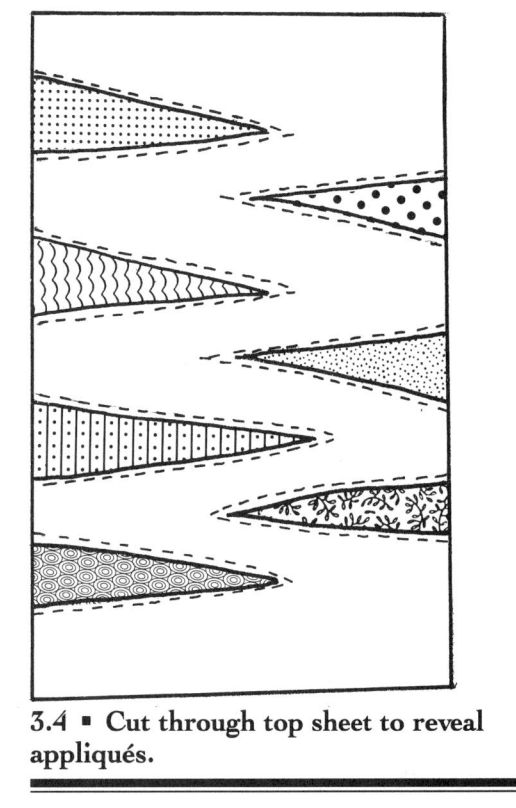

3.4 ▪ Cut through top sheet to reveal appliqués.

reverse appliqué with edge strips to hide the raw edges.

Place the bonded batting over the sheet that won't show and pin together at the top and one side. Stitch the batting and sheet together at the top and side you pinned; then remove the pins.

Cut each of seven pieces of fabric as shown and place these strips on top of the batting. Not all areas of the batting will be covered yet. Smooth and pin in place with quilting pins. Place the patchwork presser foot at the edge of the strips and straight stitch (stitch length 4) both sides to the batting and batting sheet.

Place a second sheet topside down on a flat surface (this is the topsheet that will show). Over that place the appliquéd sheet, with appliqués face down. Smooth the sheets as you pin them together with safety pins. Place the pins away from the stitched lines so you don't have to remove them as you sew.

Take the pinned sheets to your sewing machine, with appliquéd sheet still on top. Place your presser foot slightly inside the stitching lines of the triangle shapes. Stitch around (stitch length normal), following the stitching lines that hold the colored appliqués to the sheet.

When completed, remove the pins and flip the quilt over. Carefully cut through the top sheet inside the shapes to reveal the colored areas. Then place a yardstick along one edge of each strip, extending it beyond the point and to the other side. Draw a line with the

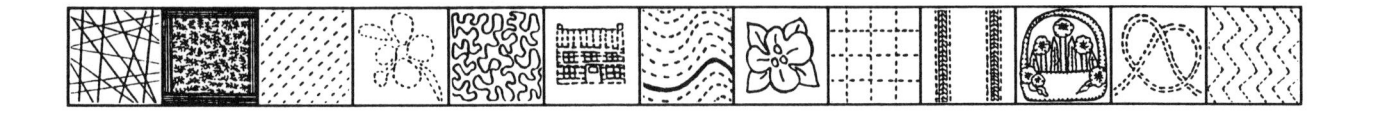

disappearing marker along the edge of the yardstick.

Cut 3" (7.5cm)-wide strips of the contrasting fabric. The strips don't have to be cut on the bias, so cut across the width of the fabric to save fabric. You will need three strips for each color. Stitch two of the strips together. To do this, place the two strips together, *both right side up.* Cut across the top on an angle (Fig. 3.6). Then sew them, right sides together, to create a more attractive slanted seam with bulk eliminated. With right sides together, sew all these strips into tubes. If you have access to the Fasturn presser foot accessory, then use it for stitching tubes together—it saves so much time. Turn the tubes right side out—the Fasturn tools make turning these a breeze—and take them to the ironing board to press flat, the seam in the center back.

Take one long and one short tube of different colors, and pin them on either side of a different color appliqué. First apply the short tube along one side just over the stitched line. Then place the longer piece on the other side, extending it to the opposite edge on top of the marked line. Use a glue stick to hold the tubes in place. Don't glue all the tubes at one time; work on only one color at a time.

While you have the quilt on a flat surface, draw in quilting lines on the top sheet using a yardstick and disappearing pen. Instead of measuring specific distances from the appliquéd bindings, draw in quilting lines wher-

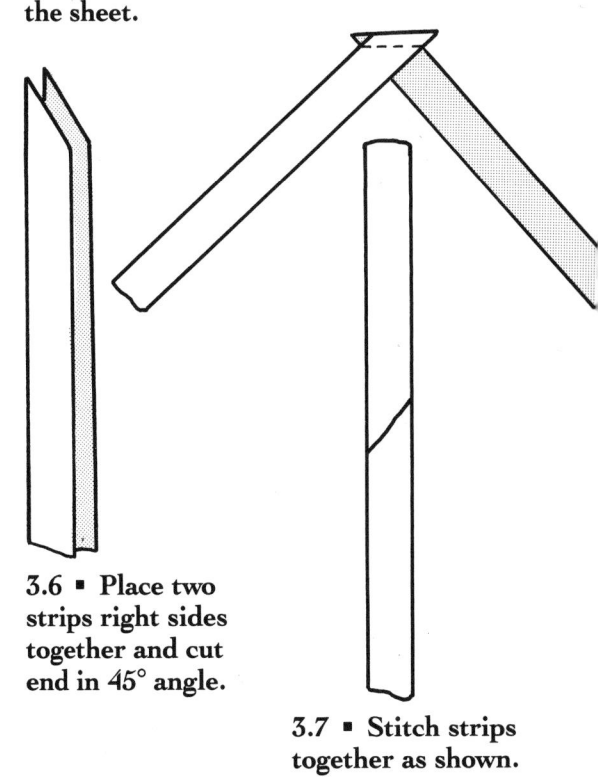

3.5 ▪ Draw guidelines from appliqués across to the other side of the sheet.

3.6 ▪ Place two strips right sides together and cut end in 45° angle.

3.7 ▪ Stitch strips together as shown.

ever you think they're needed. Echo the shapes made by the bindings, and add straight lines as well.

Change to an open embroidery foot (it's important to see exactly where the needle is) and use clear monofilament thread on the needle. Use a blind hem stitch, needle position 5, stitch width 1½, stitch length normal for blind hem, or whatever setting you prefer for your machine. Roll up the quilt and use safety pins to hold the roll in place, leaving visible only the shapes that you're working on. Place the roll between the needle and sewing machine. Feed the quilt off the left of the machine. Place the toe of the presser foot at the outside edge of the bound shape. The needle drops into a notch in the inside of the toe, keeping the straight stitching on the sheet if you maneuver the presser foot in the right place. The bite is wide, so the edge strip is attached firmly, yet is relatively invisible if you use clear monofilament thread. Stitch down one side of the strip. To stitch the other side, change to mirror image, needle position 0. Continue stitching both sides of each edge strip, unrolling the quilt and repinning until you've completed the entire quilt.

Roll up the quilt again and pin. Change to the walking foot and finish quilting the top. Use thread the same color as the sheet.

Now trim and clean up the quilt top. Check to see that the top is squared up at corners. Finish the top edge by using the serpentine stitch or zigzag, or serge the

3.8 ▪ **Place tubes just over the appliqués' cut edges and stitch in place.**

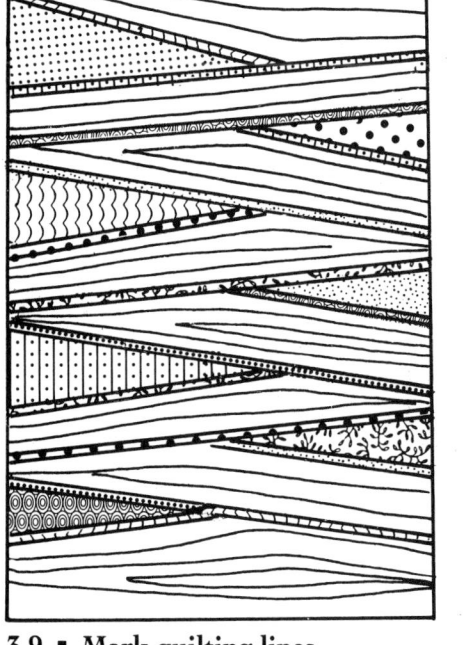

3.9 ▪ **Mark quilting lines.**

edges of the three layers together. Then fold under the top edge of the quilt top 2″ (5cm), press, and pin in place.

Stitch across on the edge. Next, place a strip of Velcro (hook side) under the edge, starting and ending 2″ (5cm) from the sides. Sew around the Velcro to attach it.

Attach the other side of the Velcro strip to the underside of the top edge of the third sheet as you did the first. Cut four 2″ (5cm) Velcro strips and sew them on the underside of the bottom sheet within the corners and at each side under the top hem. The Velcro strips hook to those we will place on the duvet to keep it from shifting in the cover.

Spread the third sheet on a flat surface, right side up. Place the quilted sheet on top, right side down, matching top and bottom edges. Smooth the sheet and quilt top, starting at the top and one edge. Pin the two layers together. Machine stitch or serge around the three sides, leaving the top open. If you've used machine stitching, then go back and use a serpentine stitch or zigzag stitch along the edge.

Once stitched, turn the duvet cover to the right side.

Stitch the other side of the 2″ (5cm) strips of Velcro under the corners of the duvet.

Insert the duvet (press the Velcro strips together), then match up and press the Velcro together at the top opening.

Cool nights or cold, you're prepared.

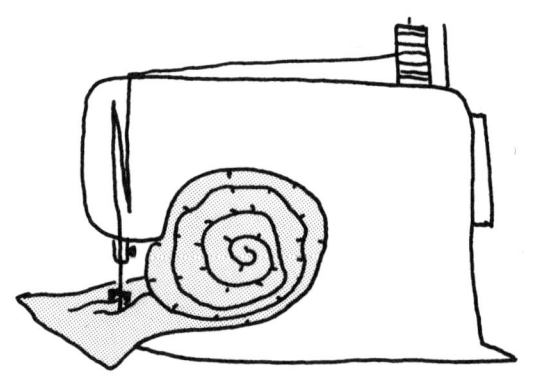

3.10 ▪ **Let quilt feed off to the left of the machine.**

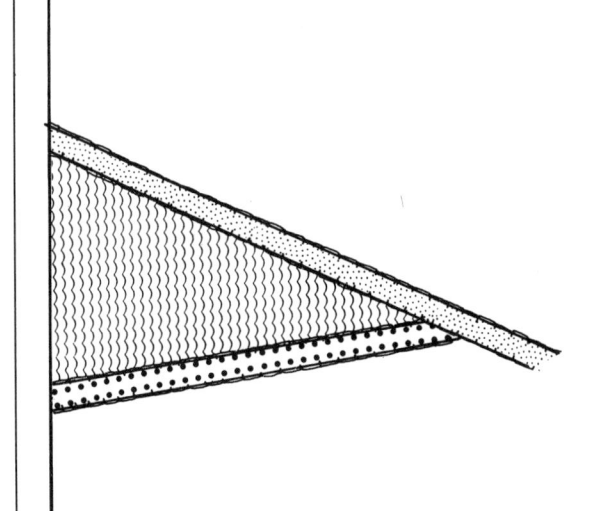

3.11 ▪ **Use blind-hem stitch to attach strips on either side of the appliqués.**

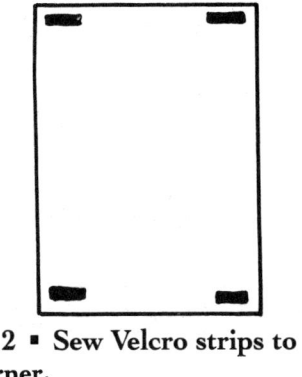

3.12 ▪ **Sew Velcro strips to each corner.**

YOU WILL NEED:

Fabric: scraps from duvet cover to cover pillow top 20″ x 26″ (51cm × 66cm); backing piece 24½″ × 26½″ (62.2cm × 66cm); stiff, heavy fabric (I used red denim) for edging (3½″ × 97″ [9cm × 2.5m])

Thread: polyester sewing to match edging, clear monofilament

Needle: #80/12

Presser Foot: zigzag (0), patchwork (37), walking foot (50) (optional)

Miscellaneous: standard bed pillow; fleece slightly larger than top; rotary cutter and mat; 6″ × 24″ (15cm × 61cm) clear plastic ruler; silver quilting pencil; small piece of template plastic; 1″ × 52″ (2.5cm × 1.3cm) fusible web; 1″ × 24″ (2.5cm x 61cm) strip of Velcro; 1½″ × 97″ (4cm × 2.5m) strip of Lite HeatnBond

3.13 ▪ **Patchwork pillow sham.**

Confetti Pillow Sham

Gather up all the small scraps you have left over from the duvet cover. Your assignment is to sew them all together into one large piece of fabric made up of erratically arranged scraps. Nothing is planned ahead of time—and the quilting is all simple stitch-in-the-ditch.

First place all the fabric scraps in piles according to size. Then place right sides together in sets of two and seam one edge in each set, using the patchwork foot. If you have a serger, this is a good time to use it—the back of your work will be so neat— and you can accomplish the task in record time.

Try to keep the pieces squared up into squares or rectangles as you work. For example, if one piece is wider at one end than the other, then sew it to another that is wider at the opposite end. Place the edge of the patchwork presser foot on the edge of the fabric you're stitching. This makes stitching faster because you don't have to keep an eye on a seam gauge. Leave one or two scraps unattached as you'll need to sew in odd pieces later.

Once your fabric pieces are sewn together into different-sized squares and rectangles, press the seams to one side. Place the pieced

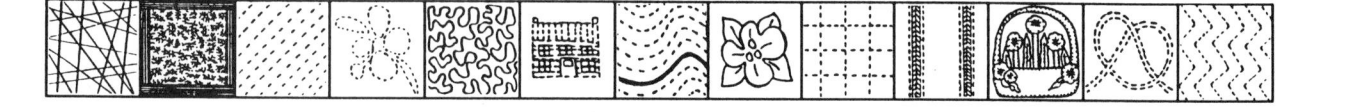

fabrics on your cutting mat. Use the rotary cutter and clear plastic ruler to square up the edges. Now slice these pieces in half the long way. Then sew the strips together to make longer strips of fabric. If your strip is 4″ (10.2cm) wide or more, cut it in half again.

Cut out several 2″ (5.1cm)-wide strips of coordinating plain fabric the same length as one of your pieced strips. Sew these to one side of each long strip. Then sew the strips together (print/plain, then print/plain, and so on).

Once you've assembled all the fabrics into larger pieces, take them to the ironing board and press them.

Now the fun begins. Take your stacks of pieced fabrics to a table and arrange them to make a 20″ × 26″ (51cm × 66cm) pillow top. If possible, plan so that no two scraps of the same fabric appear next to each other. Cut some strips in half and turn one half around or use the extra fabrics you put aside to fill in between two of the same colors. Keep cutting and arranging until the top looks unplanned, which is exactly what it is.

Use the patchwork foot to stitch the pieces together with ¼″ (6mm) seam allowances. When the pillow top is the right size, press it well again.

Then place the pillow top on the mat, and use a rotary cutter and ruler to square the edges.

Pin the scrappy top to a piece of Pellon fleece (slightly larger than the top). Stitch-in-the-ditch down the longest seams to hold the Pellon in place so you can remove the

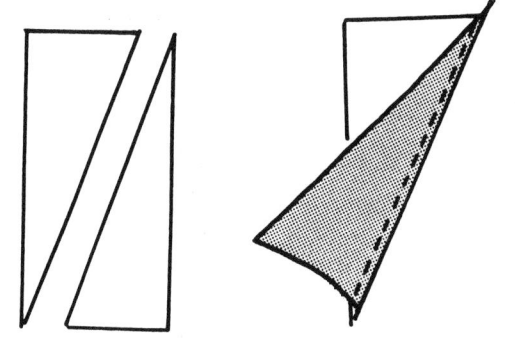

3.14 ▪ Sew scraps together into squares and rectangles.

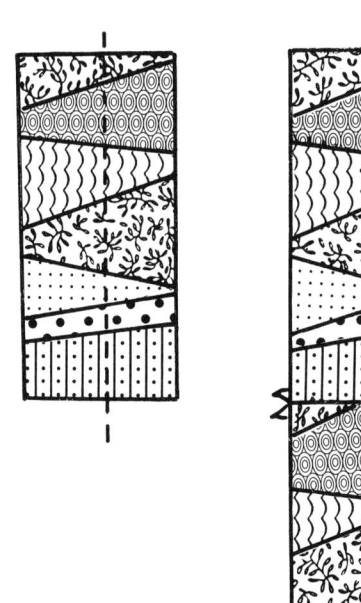

3.15 ▪ Sew scraps into strips; then cut each in two and sew the two together into a longer strip.

3.16 ▪ **Sew plain strips between scrap strips.**

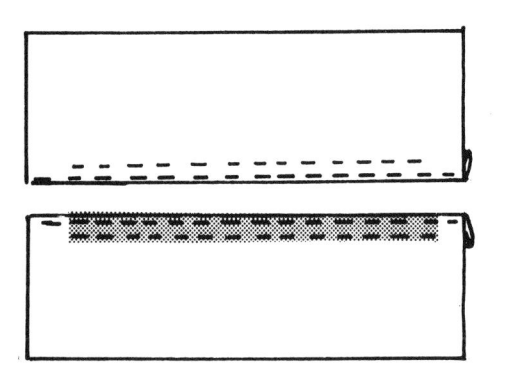

3.17 ▪ **Stitch Velcro at each side of the backing.**

pins. Go back and stitch in some, or all, of the remaining seams. Clean up the edges to remove any protruding fleece. Put the pillow top aside.

Use Velcro for the opening. First cut out two pieces of backing fabric—choose a fabric to match one of the scraps on the top. Each piece of backing is cut 26″ × 12¼″ (66cm × 30.8cm). To prepare the opening, press a 1″ (2.5cm) strip of fusible web underneath the long edge of both pieces of fabric. After removing the paper, fold the edges under 1″ (2.5cm) and fuse them by pressing with an iron. Then fold them again, press, and pin to hold them while stitching.

Stitch both fabrics along the first fold of each piece. Next, starting 1″ (2.5cm) from the edge, align the hook side of the Velcro tape at the stitching line under the top edge, with the other side of the Velcro on the top edge of the other side of the backing. Stitch down the two long sides of each Velcro strip.

Press the two sides of the Velcro together and line up the edges above and below the tape so these can be sewn down. Sew together by continuing the Velcro stitching lines from the Velcro to the edge on both sides. Put the back of the sham aside until the decorative edging is attached to the front of the top.

Use a heavy coordinating fabric for the edging. You may piece the edging if necessary.

After cutting a 3½″ (9cm)-wide strip for each side of the pillow top, fold the strips the long way, wrong sides together, and lay a

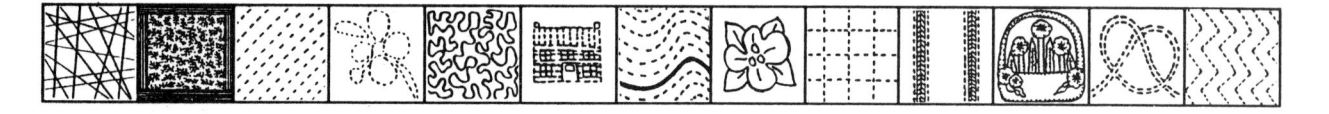

1½″ (3.8cm) strip of Lite HeatnBond at the cut edge inside one side. Fuse. Remove the paper, fold the strip again, and do the final fuse.

Use a ruler and silver quilting pencil to mark a line ¼″ (6mm) from the folded edge of each strip. This is the stitching line. Then cut a triangle template from clear plastic. Place the point at the fused edge and use a silver quilting pencil to mark the pointy edging across each strip. Stitch just inside the marked line and cut out the triangles on the marked lines.

Prepare one side at a time. Center a strip on one edge of the front of the pillow top matching cut edges with folded edge of strip, and pin. Finish each side in the same way. Stitch in place on the marked seam line.

Next, sew the pillow together. Place right sides of backing and top together. Stitch from the top to follow the edging stitching lines. Trim the corners. Then pull the Velcro open and turn the pillow right side out. Slip the pillow form inside and close again.

OPTIONAL:

Stitch Pellon fleece to the inside back, too. By backing pillowcases with batting, the pillowcases look smoother.

3.18 ▪ **Mark a line ¼″ (6mm) from the folded edge.**

¼″ (6cm)

1½″ (4cm)

3.19 ▪ **Make a triangle template from this pattern.**

1½″ (4cm)   1½″ (4cm)   1½″ (4cm)   ¼″ (6m)

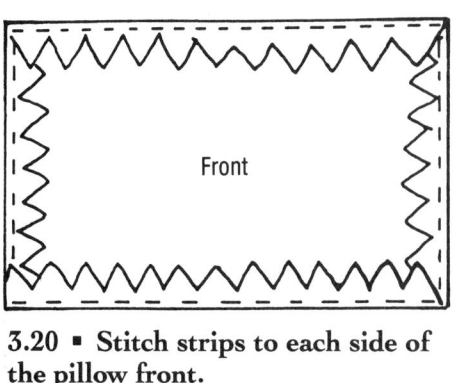

Front

3.20 ▪ **Stitch strips to each side of the pillow front.**

YOU WILL NEED:

Fabric: red tulle (8″ × 6″ [20.5cm × 15cm]); red and green plaid cotton (8″ × 3″ [20.5cm × 7.5cm]), bright blue cotton (4″ × 3″ [10cm × 7.5cm]), red and white striped ticking (9″ × 7″ [23cm × 17cm]), basket-like fabric 1½″ × 3½″ (4cm × 9cm), blue and white snowflake print fabric, your choice of scraps (green, red, blue, yellow, and chartreuse; plain, print, and pin dot)

Needle: #80/12, hand-sewing for pearl cotton

Thread: clear monofilament; red, green, blue pearl cotton or cotton machine embroidery thread

Presser foot: zigzag (0), free-embroidery (24)

Miscellaneous: red picture frame (5″ × 7″ [13cm x 17cm]) with cardboard insert (or cut your own); thick tacky glue; glue stick; single-edge razor blade; brown wrapping paper (9″ × 7″ [23cm × 18cm]); several small nails; two screw eyes; and wire for hanging

Flower Basket Collage

Most of us grew up turning under appliqué edges and tacking them in place invisibly. I'm glad I've changed my ways, or I'd have to leave out this small collage. These colorful pictures make one-of-a-kind gifts that are simple to make and wonderful to receive. Although you'll never find the same fabrics I worked with, let's pretend you do—explanations are easier this way—as I walk you through my favorite way to appliqué.

This basket of flowers is ablaze with primary colors: red, blue, yellow, with bright green and a bit of chartreuse thrown in for good measure.

Before I began, I chose appropriate fabrics (you can use scraps for this small picture if you have them). Included are pin dots of red, green, and blue; solids of yellow and blue; red with big white polka dots, green with small yellow, red, and blue flowers. I was lucky to find white fabric with a wide green grid over it, which gives a woven basket effect. Then I chose to add three lace motifs (I cut them out of a larger piece of lace). Also, I cut out four smaller circles from the same piece of lace.

I used a red frame, removing the glass, leaving the embroidery uncovered.

3.21 ▪ Flower basket collage.

To make the background fabric, cut out and place the red and white ticking on the cardboard. Next cut out the piece of bright blue fabric and place this at the right on top of the ticking (place a dot of glue under the blue fabric to hold it in place temporarily). Red plaid fabric covers the bottom part of the picture and overlaps the blue fabric. Remove the cardboard and sew the sections together by stitching at the edge of the blue fabric and across the top edge of the plaid fabric with clear monofilament.

Place this background fabric on top of the cardboard again and place the red frame lightly on top. Move the background fabric so the red plaid is 2″ (5cm) high, the blue fabric 2½″ (6cm) wide. Now push the cardboard into the frame and trim away the edges of fabric, leaving enough around all sides to glue in place later. Leave the frame on the background while you arrange the flower basket. Cut out the basket from a piece of fabric 1½″ x 3½″ (4cm × 9cm).

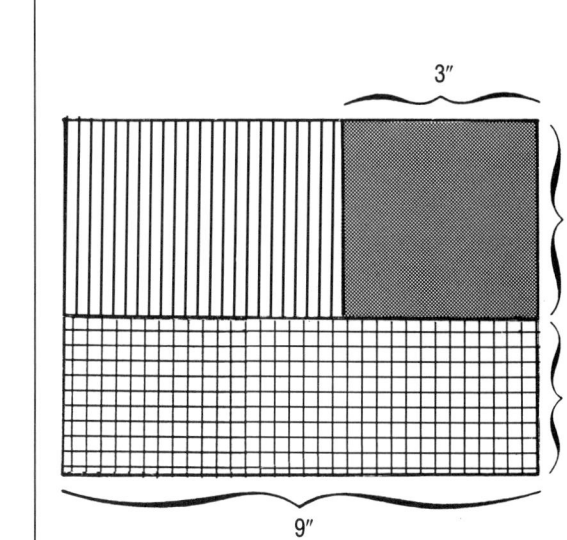

3.22 ▪ Place blue and plaid fabric on red ticking to create a background.

Now begin cutting out flowers and leaves, overlapping and building up a basket of flowers. They are all freely cut. The red polka dot fabric is cut in a circle so you can see the large white dot in the center (there are 3 of these).

Cut a circle around the white snowflake on the blue-and-white print fabric (there are 5 of these).

Place the leaves first. Cut them out of green pin dot as well as blue pin dot, yellow, and green flowered fabric. Arrange flowers (circles of red polka dot, blue and white snowflake, and lace motifs) over the leaves. Once it is in a pleasing arrangement, take the frame off. Place red tulle (bridal veil) over the collage. Pin it in place around the edges as well as pinning the pieces of the bouquet in place (it's not necessary to pin each flower or leaf).

Now take the collage to your sewing machine. Set up your machine for free machining by lowering the feed dogs and placing the free-embroidery foot on the machine.

Stitch around each motif with monofilament—just outside the edge of each shape. If the stitching runs on to the leaf or petal it's fine, since it won't show. Remember to remove the pins before you get to them. Smooth out the tulle as you stitch the veil. Once you have finished stitching the collage, stitch all around the edge of the picture—just outside where the frame will be. Draw lines in chalk if you need a guideline for stitching. Now go back and cut out the tulle over the ticking and over other areas if you wish (be

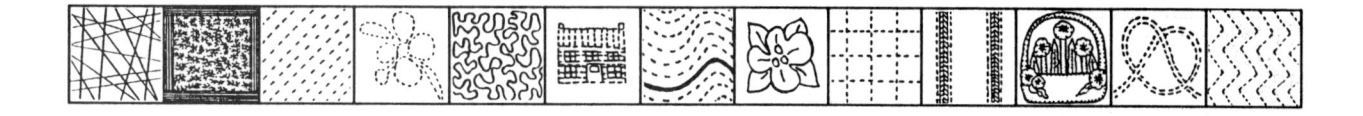

sure there is stitching there to hold the appliqués on). This isn't necessary, but it gives an added color and dimension to your picture.

If you wish, add hand embroidery with pearl cotton or free embroidery using cotton machine-embroidery thread. If you hand embroider, use only straight stitches and French knots. In the polka dot centers, stitch green snowflakes. Place red French knots in the center of each small lace circle.

You'll need some stems. Use blue for the stems and place green French knots as buds. I also added red sprigs in four different places.

If you are machine embroidering, build up blobs of thread for French knots by stitching in one place many times. Use star flowers (see Project 3, Victorian Pillows, page 26) for the green snowflakes, and make stems of narrow (stitch width 1 or 1½) satin stitches.

Embroider your initials on last. Then place the collage into the frame. Use tacky glue on the underside edges of the fabric and press them to the back of the cardboard.

Tack a few nails around the inside of the frame to hold your embroidery in place. Then cover the back edge of the frame with tacky glue, place it on top of a piece of heavy brown wrapping paper—even a grocery bag works—and press down while cutting the paper away at the edge with a single-edge razor blade. This hides the messy picture back and makes the project look professional.

Use small screw eyes and wire for hanging your masterpiece.

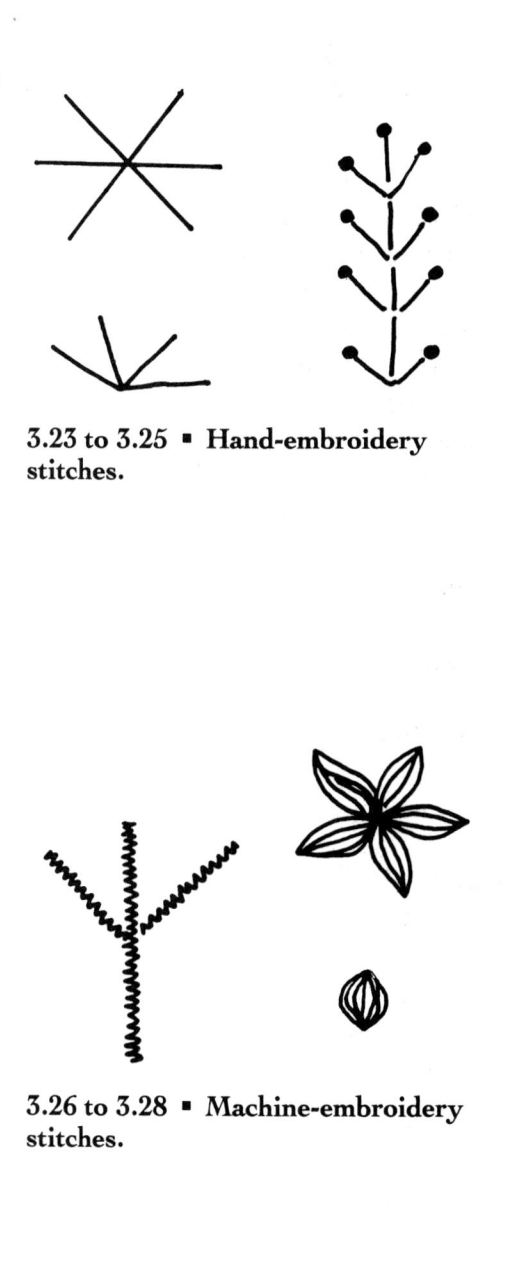

3.23 to 3.25 ▪ Hand-embroidery stitches.

3.26 to 3.28 ▪ Machine-embroidery stitches.

YOU WILL NEED:

Fabric: black denim (4 yards [3.7m]) for backing and binding; red denim (½ yard [46cm]) for four strips between the polka dot and ant fabrics; ant fabric (1¾ yards [1.5m]) or red and white checked tablecloth fabric for widest strips; black and white polka dot laminated fabric (1 yard [.91m]) for center square and pockets

Needle: #90/14 jeans (sharp), hand-sewing

Thread: clear monofilament, black polyester sewing

Presser foot: zigzag (0), jeans foot (8) (optional), free-quilting (28), free-embroidery (24), walking (50), Teflon (52)

Miscellaneous: low-loft bonded batting; one package black folded braid; safety pins; rotary cutter and mat; 6″ × 24″ (15cm × 61cm) ruler; white marking pen, chalk marking pencil, disappearing marker

Picnic Mat

What's the last thing you throw into the car when you leave for a picnic? The oldest, usually ugliest, blanket you own? Not this time. The fabric inspired me—big black ants on a red and white checked picnic tablecloth. It's perfect for a picnic blanket/tablecloth stitched into one. The tablecloth fabric, as well as the rest of the mat, is pieced, log-cabin style (courthouse steps), and then quilted, using several methods.

Before I bought enough laminated fabric for the tablecloth (the label said "wipe off to clean"), I tested it to be sure I could launder it like the rest of the mat—in the washing machine and dryer. I bought ⅛ yard

3.29 ▪ Picnic Mat.

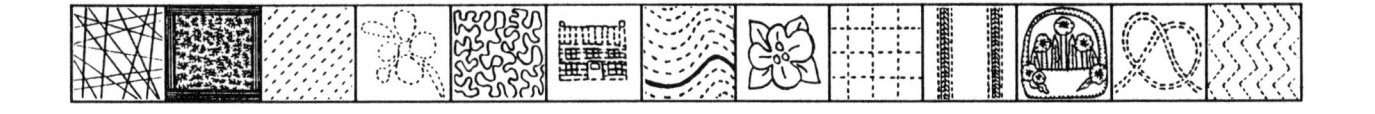

(11.4cm), washed and dried it on a cool setting, and discovered it laundered well.

Cut out the center 30" (76cm) square of laminated fabric, batting, and black denim for the backing. Cut four silverware pockets from the laminated fabric, too: 3½" × 10½" (4cm x 26cm).

When you cut out the remaining sections, cut only the width of the strips: red and black denim (four each 4½" [11.5cm]-wide strips cut across the 45" (1.1m)-wide fabrics); ant fabric and black denim (four each 10½" [26cm]-wide strips cut the length of the fabrics). Cut out batting for each piece also.

Cut black denim binding: four strips 6" × 60" [15cm × 1.5m) (these can be pieced). Cut exact lengths of each strip only after the strips are sewn to the mat.

Before stitching the center square together with batting and denim, draw quilting lines on the square of laminated fabric with a white marking pen. Then slip the square of batting between the top and black denim and pin with safety pins to baste it together. With the black thread, quilt the square with a walking foot or Teflon foot by straight stitching from corner to corner and then inside each of the four triangles formed by the diagonal lines. When finished, stitch all around the square, ¼" (6.4mm) from the edge, to hold the layers together for the next step. Trim away any batting or threads protruding from the edges.

Place a strip of red denim (right sides together) at the top edge of the laminated,

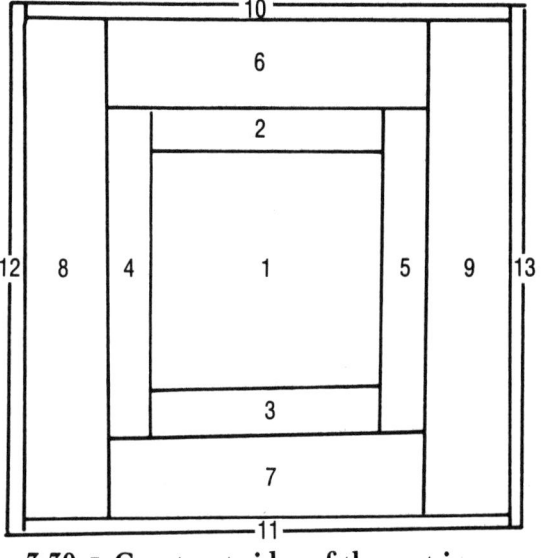

3.30 ▪ **Construct sides of the mat in this order.**

3.31 ▪ **Draw in quilting lines.**

3.32 ▪ **Stitch around the edge to attach the three layers together.**

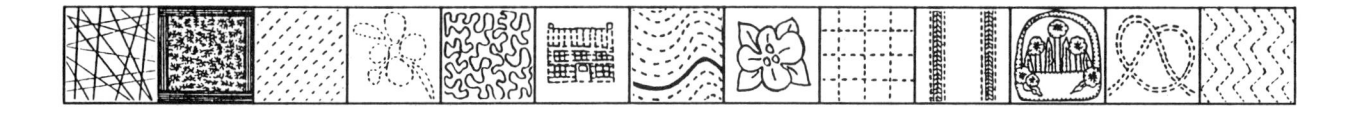

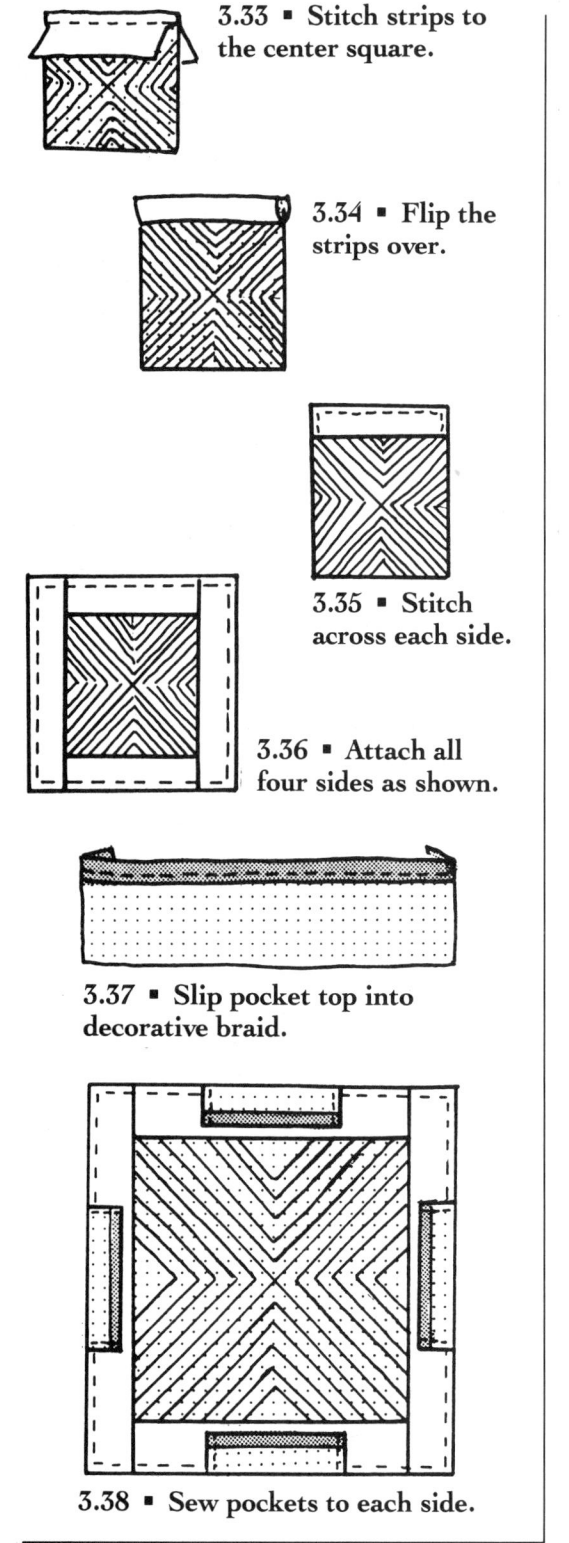

3.33 ▪ Stitch strips to the center square.

3.34 ▪ Flip the strips over.

3.35 ▪ Stitch across each side.

3.36 ▪ Attach all four sides as shown.

3.37 ▪ Slip pocket top into decorative braid.

3.38 ▪ Sew pockets to each side.

quilted square. Add a strip of black denim right sides together underneath the edge of the black denim middle square. Straight stitch together with a zigzag foot or jeans foot ½″ (13mm) from the edge (use ½″ [13mm] for all seam allowances). Flip both strips open and finger press flat. (Use an iron to press all the other strips flat, but the lamination on the center square precludes your using an iron on this fabric.) Slip in a strip of batting, pin together, and carefully cut the strip off the same length as the center square. Stitch the long and short edges closed. Trim off extra batting. Do the same at the opposite bottom side of the square.

Finish stitching the other two sides as you did the first. Stitch again at the edges to hold the strips together for the next step.

Prepare the four silverware pockets by stitching ¼″ (6.4mm) at each short side to mark fold lines. Then slip the top of each pocket into folded braid. Fold the pocket under at each short end on the stitching lines and stitch across the braid edge to hold it in place. Use glue stick sparingly where needed to hold the edges in place.

Find the centers of each pocket and mark with a pin. Then on the center square you're building, mark the center bottom of each red strip with a pin and, matching the marks, pin the pockets in place on the red strips, matching the bottom edges. Stitch down both short sides of each pocket (the bottom is caught in the seam at the bottom edge later).

Change the machine to free-machine stitching by lowering the feed dogs and

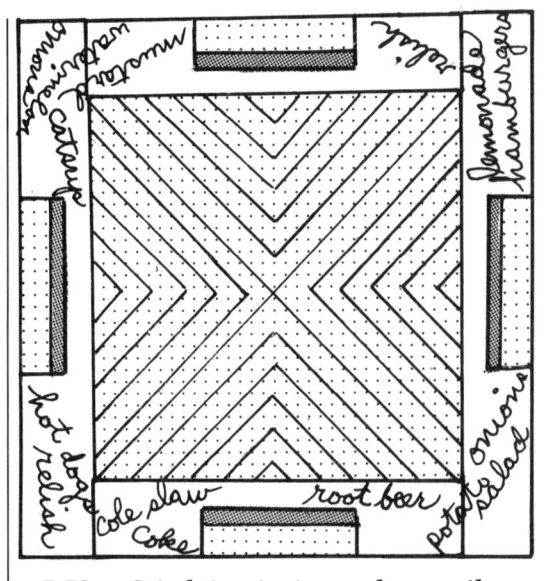

changing to the free-embroidery presser foot.

Use a disappearing marker to write picnic words on the red strips. Here are some of the words I chose: BRATS AND BEER, HAMBURG- ERS, HOT DOGS, LEMONADE, WATER- MELON, PAPER PLATES, MATCHES, GRILL, CATSUP, RELISH, MUSTARD. Check food ads in the newspaper for inspiration.

Stitch freely, using black polyester sewing thread, quilting the red strip as you stitch in the words. This is not hard to do, and you don't need a hoop if you hold the fabric taut (across the embroidery area you're stitching) as you quilt.

Next, add the ant fabric, batting, and denim as you did the red strips. The first two ant strips are attached on the same sides as the first two red strips. Follow the order in Fig. 3.30.

Once the four sides are attached and the edges sewn together, go back with the free- quilting foot or free-embroidery foot, clear monofilament thread on top and bobbin (you can use black thread in the bobbin if you wish), and stitch around the ants as you freely manipulate the fabric under the nee- dle.

Add the black denim bindings last. Fold the 6″ (15cm) strips in half, wrong side to- gether, and press. Place the first strip under- neath the mat, cut edges together, on the side you sewed the first red strip. Attach by stitching the binding ⅞″ (22mm) from the edge. Trim to neaten the edge if needed. Then pull the black denim over to the front. The fold falls slightly past the stitching line.

3.39 ▪ Stitch in picnic words to quilt the red strips.

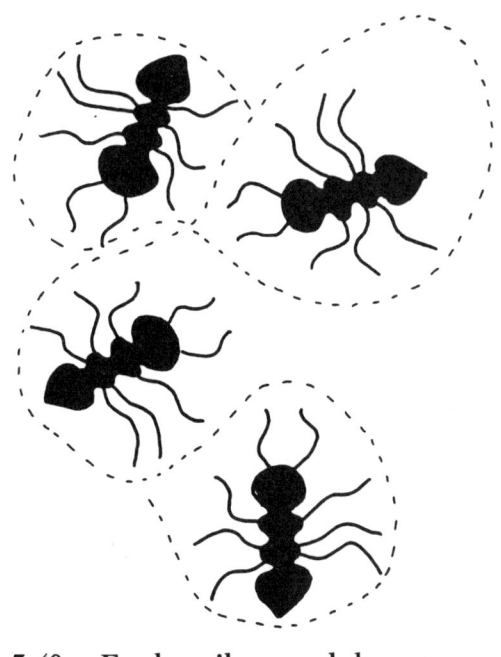

3.40 ▪ Freely quilt around the ants.

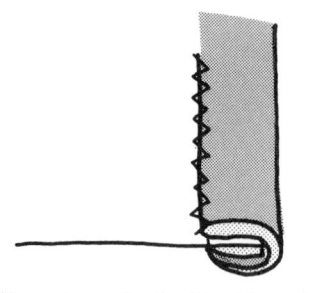

3.41 ▪ **Attach the bindings by stitching from the front.**

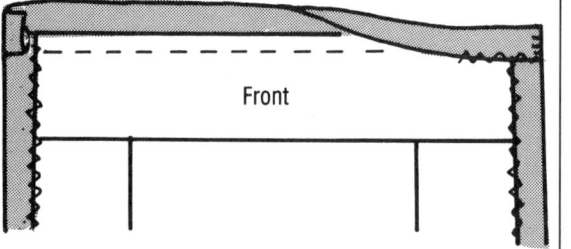

Front

3.42 ▪ **Fold under and hand-stitch ends together.**

Zigzag (stitch width 1½, stitch length 1½) on the fold with black polyester sewing thread in the bobbin and on top. Stitch the opposite side in the same way.

On the last two sides, tuck under ½″ (13cm) at both ends for a clean finish. Once attached, use a hand-sewing needle to stitch up the edges at each end.

VARIATION:

Sew on straps for carrying and add a slipcase for paper plates and napkins which you can place in the center of the mat before you fold it up for carrying.

CHAPTER 4

Quilting/ Sewing Shortcuts

Try these shortcuts and hints to help you quick-quilt and -sew:

CAN'T-DO-WITHOUT'S

Rotary cutter and mat with grid and bias; 6″ × 24″ (15cm × 61cm) clear plastic ruler (use this for a T-square, too); glue stick; thick, tacky glue (leave it uncovered and it becomes even thicker); fusibles; silver quilting pencil; vanishing markers; water-erasable markers; seam guides; Hump Jumper, for stitching over thick seams; Fasturn, for tube turning; a dowel,

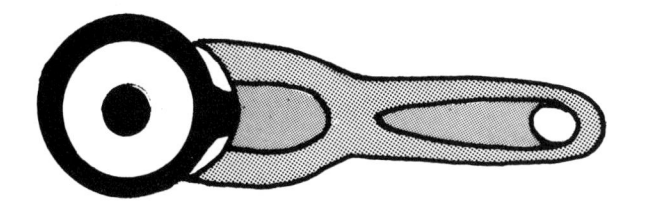

4.1 ▪ Rotary cutter.

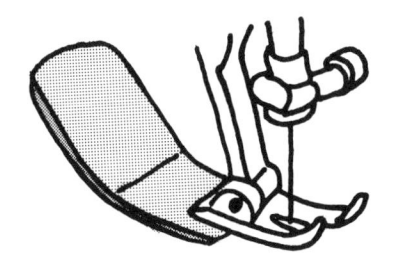

4.2 ▪ Hump Jumper.

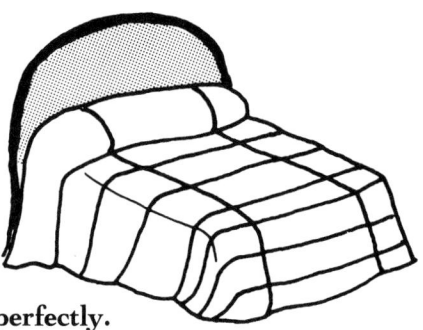

4.3 ▪ Fasturn.

4.4 ▪ **A dowel shaped for pushing out corners and stuffing dolls.**

to push out corners (one end is sanded flat like a paddle, the other is dull-pointed); and my stacks of boxes with thread, so I don't have to run out to buy thread every time I sit down to sew. (I buy monofilament thread, both clear and smoke, by the cone.)

The scissors I use most often are Fiskars 4″ pointed craft scissors and Mundial embroidery scissors. They cut all the way down to their tiny points. Also important to me are appliqué scissors (Gingher or Mundial). Most important of all are sharp cutting shears.

CLOSURES

Use Velcro for closures to save time when making a pillow. If you want a zipper closure, invisible zippers are the easiest to apply.

Use zippers-by-the-yard for odd sizes or large projects like duvet covers.

DECORATING PILLOWS AND QUILTS

A reversible pillow is like having two pillows, and it doesn't take much longer to sew. Decorate the pillow top and back differently, and leave an opening at one edge. Hand-sew closed.

If the pieces must meet perfectly, but you're afraid they won't, the best fudging trick I know is adding piping between the sections so being off a couple threads won't be noticeable (Fig. 4.5).

4.5 ▪ **Slip piping between striped fabrics to fool the eye into seeing the stripes matching perfectly.**

(But first try a walking foot, glue stick, basting tape, or fusible web strips to keep the seams in place while stitching.)

FABRIC

Use ready-mades whenever feasible: sheets for a summer quilt or duvet cover; decorated towels for rugs; or plain towels to decorate.

Use sheets for wide fabrics, but also look for extra-wide decorator fabrics in 90″ (2.3m) and 120″ (3m) widths. These are usually finish-treated, and the prints are straight on the fabric (not always true with sheets).

If a project doesn't fit across an available fabric width, check to see if you can avoid piecing by running your pattern the length of the fabric instead. (Be sure the print of the fabric is traveling in the right direction.)

Always buy more fabric than you need (don't we always?) to save possible trips to the store later. Also, fabric bought at one time will be from the same bolt and the dye lot won't vary. If you have leftovers, make napkins, wrapped baskets, patched pillows, small lap robes, even appliqués. Most of the accessories in this book are examples of projects made with small pieces of fabric.

Do you want only a hint of quilt batting? Use flannel yardage or sheets. Make bias the easy way (see Fig. 4.6–4.11).

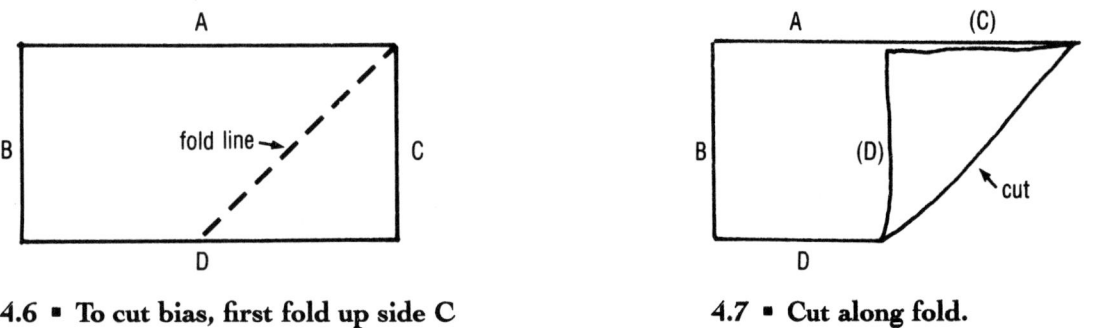

4.6 ▪ To cut bias, first fold up side C along dash line to meet side A.

4.7 ▪ Cut along fold.

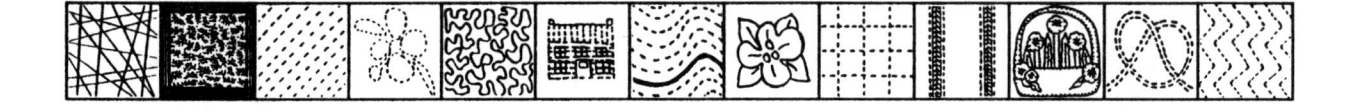

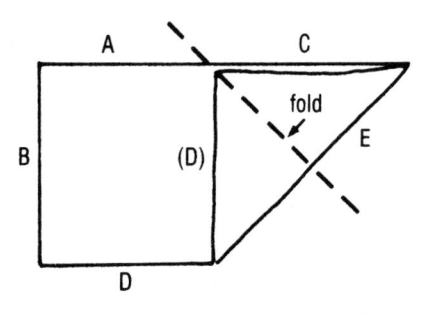

4.8 ▪ **Fold down from side C along dash line.**

4.9 ▪ **Fold again on dash line parallel to side F.**

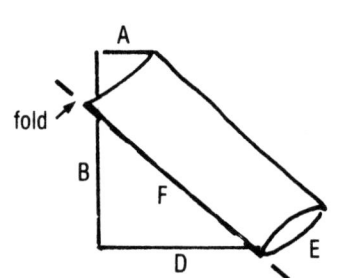

4.10 ▪ **Again, fold on dash line at F.**

cutting lines

4.11 ▪ **Cut out bias strips perpendicular to the last fold line.**

FUSIBLES AND GLUES

Use fusibles whenever possible: fleece, webbing, bonds, and tear-away stabilizers. Use iron-on freezer paper for templates. Some fusible drapery tapes, webbing, and bonds can eliminate sewing completely—wow!

Sometimes use a glue stick or dots of thick, tacky glue in place of pins, or just because there are times when they are the best choice.

Even if you buy thick, tacky glue, there are times when you need the glue thicker than thick, so do what I do: Spoon out the amount of glue needed and leave it out for an hour or as long as it takes to thicken.

Household Goop is as thick as caulk and dries clear. It is the same as the product used by jewelry makers, E6000 (but cheaper). Buy it in the hardware store and use it whenever you're afraid bulky things will shift or slide before the glue is dry.

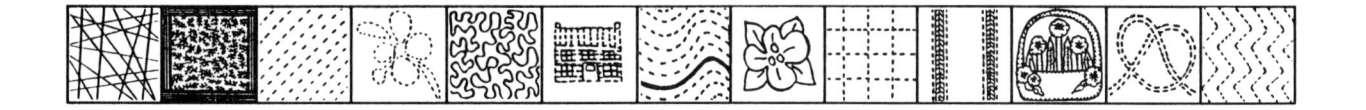

MEASURING

A rotary cutter mat with grid and bias lines is a must. So is a clear plastic ruler, 6″ × 24″ (15cm × 60.1cm).

When feasible, measure seam allowances with presser foot widths and de-centering needles (cut your fabrics to allow this seam allowance size). Lining up the presser foot edge at the edge of the fabric makes sewing a straight line easy and fast.

Use presser feet in combination with seam guides and screw-type seam guides for the bed of your machine when accuracy is a must.

To turn under a seam allowance easily, first stitch on the seam line, then turn under. This is especially helpful for ⅛″ (3mm) and ¼″ (6mm) hems.

PILLOWCASES AND PILLOW FORMS

If you need more filling in a pillow, wrap the pillow form with batting. Fill the pillowcase corners with handfuls of fiberfill.

When the pillow form is soft, cut the pillowcase the same size as the form. Then, when the ¼″ (6mm) seam allowances are sewn around the case, it reduces the pillowcase size and the form fits better. This doesn't work with thick rubber forms.

Round off pillowcase corners, or stitch 2–3 small stitches diagonally across them for a neater corner.

PIPING, WELTING, AND FRINGES

Always cover the piping and welting first, before attaching it to the edge of the pillow or quilt.

Attach piping, welting, or fringe to one side of the pillow at a time. After stitching the decoration to one side, pin to the other side, and using the stitching line as a guide, stitch the layers together slightly inside the line.

It's faster to buy covered piping, welting, and fringe by the yard, but

weigh the cost—sometimes it's not worth it. Bite the bullet and make your own. The bulky overlock (12) foot makes covering piping and welting a breeze. Check Fasturn's method of making piping. It's super-fast.

QUICK-QUILTING CONSTRUCTION

Use safety pins for basting a quilt.

If possible, work in small, easy-to-manipulate sections. If you make a large quilt, divide it into sections and quilt the sections up to the seam allowances. Later sew the seam allowances together into the large quilt.

When quilting a large sandwich of fabrics, I pull my sewing machine table away from the wall and place a large piece of Masonite on it to keep the weight of the quilt from pulling the quilt away from the needle. It saves my shoulders.

Roll the quilt, then pin the roll together or use "bicycle clips" to hold it together. Fit the roll between the sewing needle and machine. Then, as you sew, the quilt feeds off the left-hand side, so you're not dealing with bulk.

Even if you've read that you must stitch in only one direction and start from the center and go out to each side, I've never listened to this. I stitch in whichever direction is the easiest to maneuver my quilt, and I've never been disappointed with the looks of the quilt.

Though this won't make the quilt quicker, it's the hint my classes thank me for more than any other (they may be waiting for someone to give them permission): Never sit down at the machine and quilt from morning till night until you've finished the whole quilt. Instead, visually divide the quilt into sections. Make up your mind to quilt only one section a day. For example, when I make log cabin quilts, I quilt one row of squares each morning, then lay it aside till the next day and do another row. It may take me more than a week to quilt it, but when I'm done I can honestly say it was fun.

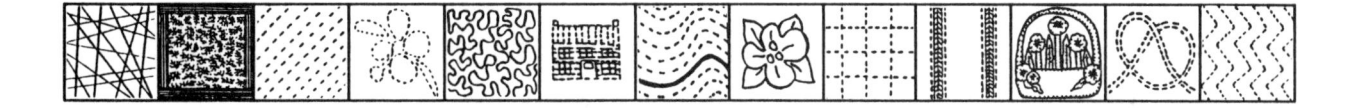

SPEED-QUILTING AND -SEWING

Quilt on printed lines on the fabric when you can.

Use striped fabric instead of piecing narrow strips of fabric together.

There are no puckers and pleats when you use a walking foot. In fact, know how to use all the specialty feet available for your machine. Use the best needle and thread for each job. And, most important, know your sewing machine!

Use your shirring foot (16) or gathering accessory to gather ruffles, but zigzag over gimp to gather them if the fabric is heavy.

Load up multiple bobbins before beginning any project.

Use a serger for construction, even for decorating the fabric such as for rolled hems, gathering, and creating practical, textures.

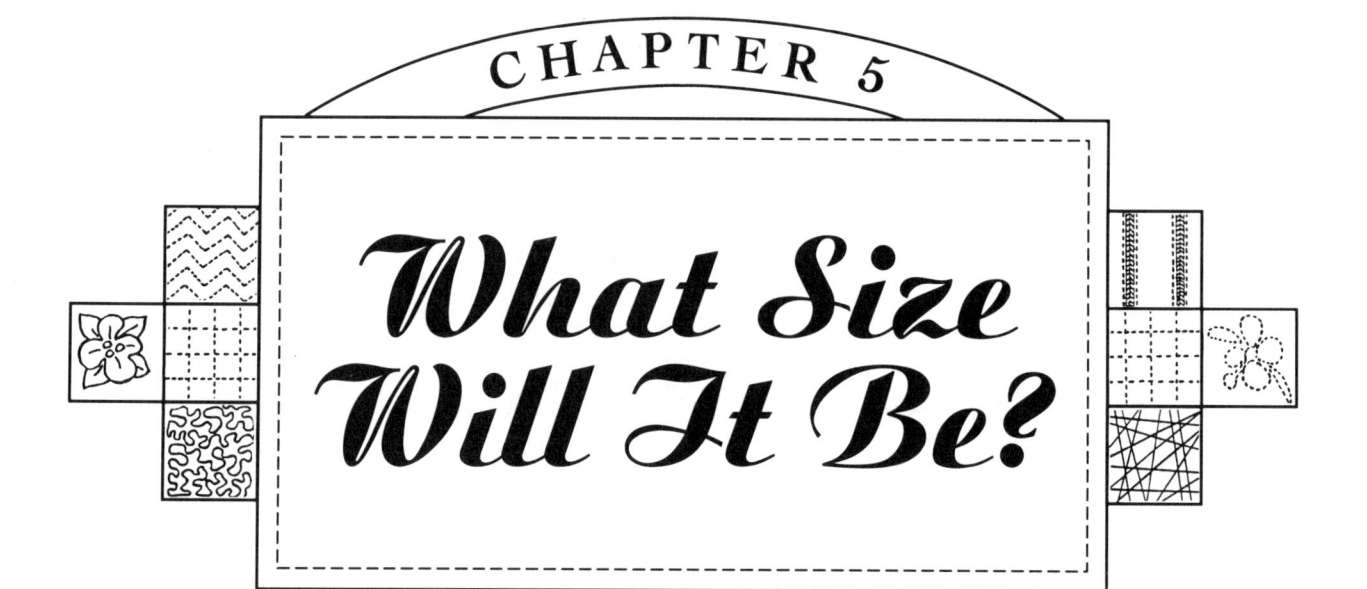

CHAPTER 5

What Size Will It Be?

When I make a quilt, I want it long enough to fit under the mattress at the foot of the bed and reach over my head at the top. Only then am I satisfied with the size. Someone once called that "wiggle room," a good word for it. I have to make one that size—a ready-made isn't available.

I have a "thing" about bedspreads, too. I want them to include enough fabric to reach the floor on three sides and fold under and turn over the pillows at the top. The fold is deep and the spread reaches to the headboard. I make bedspreads, too, because I'm never satisfied with the sizes of ready-mades. Isn't that why we all sew for our homes? We know, as sewing enthusiasts, we don't have to settle for just OK.

The charts that follow show standard sizes of beds, sheets, pillowcases, pillow forms, and tablecloths. That's a start. But if you want a longer than standard blanket, or deeper or shorter drop on a tablecloth, then make it the size you prefer.

If you want to be totally confused, check standard mattress measurements from more than one source. I consulted several different books and

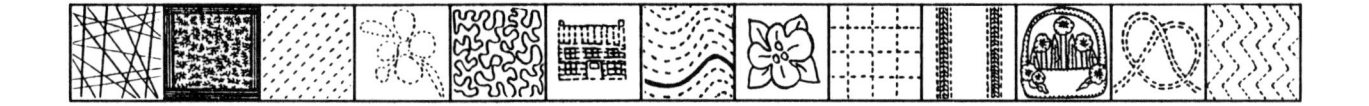

periodicals and arbitrarily chose the measurements that appeared most often on the charts (Fig. 5.1). When in doubt, measure the actual bed you're sewing for.

Standard bedding sizes are as follows:

MATTRESS

6-year crib	27″ × 52″	(68.5cm × 1.3m)
Twin	39″ × 75″	(99cm × 1.9m)
Double	54″ × 75″	(1.4m × 1.9m)
Queen	60″ × 80″	(1.5m × 2m)
King	76″ × 80″	(1.9m × 2m)
Calif. King	72″ × 84″	(1.8m × 2.2m)

FLAT SHEET

27″ × 36″	(68.5cm × .9m)
66″ × 96″	(1.7m × 2.4m)
81″ × 96″	(2m × 2.4m)
90″ × 102″	(2.3m × 2.6m)
108″ × 102″	(2.7m × 2.6m)

5.1 ▪ Mattress sizes.

The standard drop for beds is 21″ (53.5cm).

BED PILLOW SIZES

Standard	20″ × 26″	(51cm × 66cm)
Queen	20″ × 30″	(51cm × 76cm)
King	20″ × 36″	(51cm × 91.5cm)

5.2 ▪ Bed pillow sizes.

Decorative Pillow Forms: Decorative standard square pillow forms are 12″ (31cm), 14″ (36cm), 16″ (41cm), 18″ (46cm), 20″ (51cm), 26″ (66cm), 30″ (76cm). Odd shapes and sizes are available at decorator fabric shops.

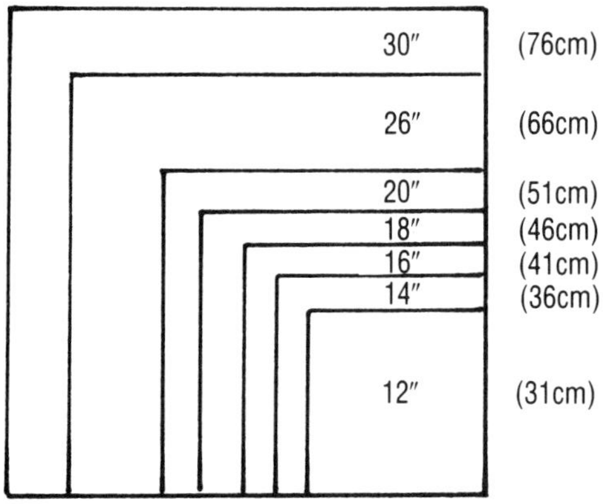

30″	(76cm)
26″	(66cm)
20″	(51cm)
18″	(46cm)
16″	(41cm)
14″	(36cm)
12″	(31cm)

5.3 ▪ Decorative pillow form sizes.

Tablecloths: Standard drop lengths are short for everyday use, 10″ (25.5cm) to 12″ (30.5cm), or long to reach the floor, approximately 29″ (73.5cm) for decorator tables.

Standard tablecloth sizes for everyday use:

52″ × 52″	(1.3m × 1.3m)
52″ × 70″	(1.3m × 1.8m)
60″ × 84″	(1.5m × 2.2m)
60″ × 120″	(1.5m × 3m)
60″ × 144″	(1.5m × 3.7m)
70″ round	(1.8m)
90″ round	(2.3m)

Standard shower curtain size: 72″ × 72″ (1.85m × 1.85m).

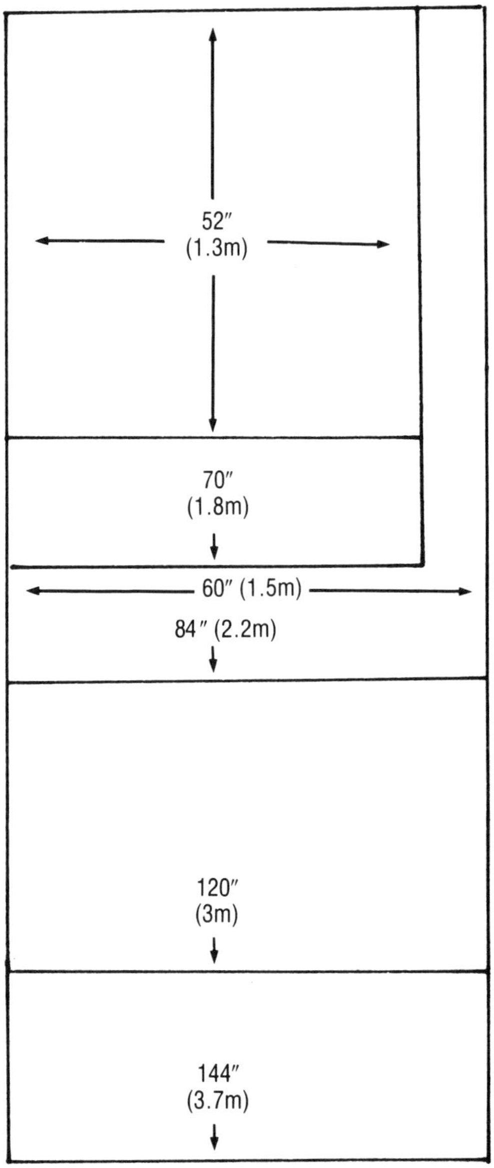

52″ (1.3m)
70″ (1.8m)
60″ (1.5m)
84″ (2.2m)
120″ (3m)
144″ (3.7m)

5.4 ▪ Standard tablecloth sizes.

Now get out a tape measure, pencil, and notebook. If you can measure, you can decorate.

AFTERWORD

When I sew, I love to experiment. I'm inspired by fabrics and threads, and when I start designing projects, it's always "What if . . . ?" Once I begin asking myself questions, one idea leads to another and another, and soon I have a stack of experiments on my sewing table. I won't use many of them; they're just part of the progression from first spark to success.

I've included some of those successes in this book. Start with them as written, or use the projects as a jumping-off place for your own experiments by changing the colors, fabrics, threads, and stitches. That's what makes home decor sewing fun. It's also fun saying, "I made it myself."

BIBLIOGRAPHY

Allen, Alice. *Sashiko Made Simple*. Hinsdale, IL: Bernina of America, 1992.

Black, Lynette Ranney, and Linda Wisner. *Creative Serging for the Home*. Portland, OR: Palmer/Pletsch Associates, 1991.

Brown, Gail. *Gail Brown's All-New Instant Interiors*. Radnor, PA: Chilton Book Co., 1992.

Cairns, Pat. *Contemporary Quilting Techniques*. Radnor, PA: Chilton Book Co., 1991.

Coleman, Ann. *Quilting New Dimensions*, London, England: Batsford Ltd., 1989.

Colvin, Maggie. *Pure Fabrication*. Radnor, PA: Chilton Book Co., 1985.

Fanning, Robbie, and Tony Fanning. *The Complete Book of Machine Quilting*. Radnor, PA: Chilton Book Co., 1980.

Finishing Touches. Radnor, PA: Chilton Book Co., 1992.

Hallock, Anita. *Fast Patch*. Radnor, PA: Chilton Book Co., 1989.

Hargrave, Harriet. *Heirloom Machine Quilting*. Lafayette, CA: C & T Publishing, 1990.

Johannah, Barbara. *Continuous Curve Quilting: Machine Quilting the Pieced Quilt*. Menlo Park, CA: Pride of the Forest, 1980.

Kinser, Charleen. *Sewing Sculpture*. NY: M. Evans and Co., Inc., 1977.

Lehman, Bonnie, and Judy Martin. *Taking the Math Out of Making Patchwork Quilts*. Wheat Ridge, CO: Moon Over the Mountain Publishing, 1981.

Moore, Nancy. *Machine-Quilted Jackets, Vests, and Coats*. Radnor, PA: Chilton Book Co., 1991.

Reader's Digest Complete Guide to Sewing. Pleasantville, NY: Reader's Digest Association, Inc., 1976.

Roberts, Sharee Dawn. *Creative Machine Art*. Paducah, KY: American Quilter's Society, 1992.

Rostocki, Janet. *Sashiko for Machine Sewing*. Dayton, OH: Summa Design, 1988.

Scott, Toni. *The Complete Book of Stuffedwork*. Boston, MA: Houghton Mifflin Co., 1978.

Short, Eirian. *Quilting Technique, Design and Application*. London, England: Batsford Ltd., 1983.

Singer Reference Library. *Sewing Projects for the Home*. Minnetonka, MN: Cy DeCosse Inc., 1991.

———. *Sewing for the Home*. 1988.

———. *More Sewing for the Home*. 1987.

Slipcovers and Bedspreads. Menlo Park, CA: Lane Publishing Co., 1983.

Solvit, Marie-Janine. *Pictures in Patchwork*. NY: Sterling Publishing Co., Inc., 1977.

Wagner, Debra. *Teach Yourself Machine Piecing and Quilting*. Radnor, PA: Chilton Book Co., 1992.

Wormleighton, Alison, ed. *Soft Furnishings for the Home*. NY: Simon & Schuster, Inc., 1985.

SOURCES OF SUPPLIES

(so that you can keep burrowing)

Aardvark Adventures, Box 2449, Livermore, CA 94550 (800/388-ANTS). A wonderful collection of unique threads (distributor of Natesh rayon machine-embroidery thread), beads, bells, kits, or you name it, for all needlepeople. There is a fantastic, free newsletter, "Aardvark Territorial Enterprise," when you become a customer. (Or subscribe for $12 with U.S. zip code; $15 foreign.) Catalog $2 (refunded with first order).

Buffalo Batt & Felt Corp., 3307 Walden Ave., Depew, NY 14043 (716/683-4100, ext. 8). Fiberfill, quilt batt, and pillow forms. Brochure with samples ($1 refundable).

Cabin Fever Calicos, P.O. Box 550106, Atlanta, GA 30355. Quilt books, notions, fabrics, batting. Send for their fabric swatches and you'll be entertained for hours.

Clotilde, Inc., 1909 SW First Ave., Ft. Lauderdale, FL 33315 (800/722-2891). Generic sewing machine feet, pearls and piping foot, threads, books, videos, needles, and notions. Free catalog.

The Crowning Touch, 2410 Glory C Rd., Medford, OR 97501 (503/772-8430). Makers of Fasturn turning tools and Fastube sewing foot, hi/low adaptor. LSASE.

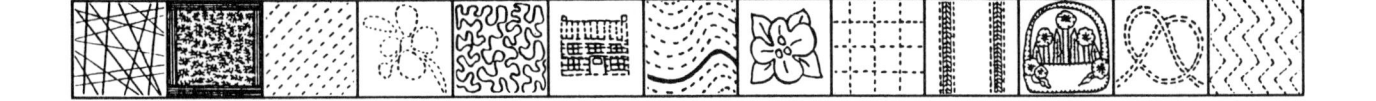

The Fabric Center, 488 Electric Ave., P.O. 8212, Fitchburg, MA 01420-8212 (508/343-4402). Discounts on most major decorator fabrics. Free brochure; 164-page catalog $2.

Fairfield Processing Corporation, 88 Rose Hill Ave., P.O. Box 1157, Danbury, CT 06813. Products include four types of fiberfill (Poly-Fil, Poly-Fil Supreme, Crafter's Choice, and EZ Stuff), four bonded and two needlepunch battings in a variety of sizes, pillow forms in firm and down-like softness, pellets for use as weighted stuffing material, and a line of patterns. Call 800/243-0989 to locate the nearest retail store in your area.

G Street Fabrics, Mail Order Service, 12240 Wilkins Ave., Rockville, MD 20852 (301/231-8960). Mail-order fabrics and custom service. They'll send swatches.

The Green Pepper, 3918 West First Ave., Eugene, OR 97402 (503/345-6665). Recreational fabrics, battings, hardware, and zippers. Catalog $2.

Home-Sew, Dept. QQ1, Bethlehem, PA 18018 (215/867-3833). Sewing notions, laces, trims, buttons, zippers, ribbons, some fabrics. Free catalog.

Kaye Wood Publishing Co., P.O. Box 456, West Branch, MI 48661 (800/248-KAYE). Quilting supplies, specialized tools, videotapes, and books. Catalog of quilting supplies $1.

Keepsake Quilting, P.O. Box 1459, Meredith, NH 03253 (603/253-8731). Send for their catalog, which includes notions, fabrics, books, and batting.

Kunin Felt—a Foss Mfg. Co., 380 Lafayette Rd., P.O. Box 5000, Hampton, NH 03842 (800/233-3358). Manufacturer of 100% polyester colored felt. Wholesale, but they will answer your questions and direct you to stores in your area that sell their felt.

Madeira Marketing, Ltd., 600 East Ninth St., Michigan City, IN 46360 (800/275-9003 or 219/873-1000). High-quality yarns, threads, and flosses. LSASE.

Nancy's Notions, Ltd., P.O. Box 683, Beaver Dam, WI 53916 (800/833-0690). Books, videos, notions, glues, machine accessories, wide-width decorator fabrics, fusibles, Ultrasuede, and Ultrasuede scraps, pearls and piping foot. Free catalog.

National Thread & Supply, 695 Red Oak Rd., Stockbridge, GA 30281. Name-brand sewing supplies and notions. Free catalog.

Newark Dressmaker Supply, P.O. Box 20730, Lehigh Valley, PA 18002-0730. Pleating and shirring tapes, decorator fabrics, sewing notions, decorative threads, trims, and laces. Free catalog.

Oregon Tailor Supply, P.O. Box 42284, Portland, OR 97242 (800/678-2457). Notions and threads. LSASE.

Pacific Fabrics Shop at Home, P.O. Box C3637, Seattle, WA 98124 (800/446-6710). Lampshade frames, fabrics, notions.

Quilters' Resource, Inc., P.O. Box 148850, Chicago, IL 60614. Lamés, threads, kits, buttons, and braids you won't see anywhere else.

Quilting Books Unlimited, 1911 W. Wilson, Batavia, IL 60510 (708/406-0237). Large selection of quilt-related books. Catalog $1.

Quilts & Other Comforts, Box 394, 6700 W. 44th Ave., Wheat Ridge, CO 80034-0394. Publishers of *Quilter's Newsletter Magazine* and *Quiltmaker*, their catalog contains fabric, patterns, templates, books, and kits. Catalog $2.50.

Sew Art International, P.O. Box 550, Bountiful, UT 84010. Unusual threads.

Sew/Fit Co., 5768 West 77th Street, Burbank, IL 60459 (800/547-ISEW). For local or Canadian calls—708/458-5600. Notions, cutting tools, and mats. Free catalog.

Speed Stitch, 3113 Broadpoint Drive, Harbor Heights, FL 33983 (800/874-4115). Sulky rayon and metallics, invisible threads, machine-embroidery supplies, and kits. Catalog $3 (refundable with order).

Treadleart, 25834 Narbonne Ave., Lomita, CA 90717 (800/327-4222). Decorative and utility machine threads, notions, books, patterns. Bimonthly magazine. Catalog $3.

INDEX